HOW TO SURVIVE
IN TUDOR
ENGLAND

*If you can keep your head when all about you
Are losing theirs and blaming it on you…*

'If' by Rudyard Kipling, c.1895

HOW TO SURVIVE IN TUDOR ENGLAND

TONI MOUNT

PEN & SWORD
HISTORY
AN IMPRINT OF PEN & SWORD BOOKS LTD.
YORKSHIRE – PHILADELPHIA

First published in Great Britain in 2023 by
PEN AND SWORD HISTORY
An imprint of
Pen & Sword Books Ltd
Yorkshire – Philadelphia

Copyright © Toni Mount, 2023

ISBN 978 1 39902 328 3

The right of Toni Mount to be identified as Author of this work has been asserted by her in accordance with the Copyright, Designs and Patents Act 1988.

A CIP catalogue record for this book is available from the British Library.

All rights reserved. No part of this book may be reproduced or transmitted in any form or by any means, electronic or mechanical including photocopying, recording or by any information storage and retrieval system, without permission from the Publisher in writing.

Typeset in Times New Roman 12/16 by
SJmagic DESIGN SERVICES, India.
Printed and bound in the UK by CPI Group (UK) Ltd.

Pen & Sword Books Limited incorporates the imprints of Atlas, Archaeology, Aviation, Discovery, Family History, Fiction, History, Maritime, Military, Military Classics, Politics, Select, Transport, True Crime, Air World, Frontline Publishing, Leo Cooper, Remember When, Seaforth Publishing, The Praetorian Press, Wharncliffe Local History, Wharncliffe Transport, Wharncliffe True Crime and White Owl.

For a complete list of Pen & Sword titles please contact
PEN & SWORD BOOKS LIMITED
George House, Units 12 & 13, Beevor Street, Off Pontefract Road,
Barnsley, South Yorkshire, S71 1HN, England
E-mail: enquiries@pen-and-sword.co.uk
Website: www.pen-and-sword.co.uk

or
PEN AND SWORD BOOKS
1950 Lawrence Rd, Havertown, PA 19083, USA
E-mail: uspen-and-sword@casematepublishers.com
Website: www.penandswordbooks.com

Contents

Chapter 1	An Introduction to How to Survive in Tudor England	1
	What happened to the Plantagenets in August 1485?	2
	Setting the Scene	3
	A brief overview of Tudor history	7
Chapter 2	**Social Structure**	18
	Being poor	18
	Dealing with the poor	21
	Sturdy rogues and con-artists	23
	Going abroad	26
	Being a gentleman or lady	27
	Money	29
	London for the wealthy	33
Chapter 3	**Education and Employment Opportunities**	35
	New occupations	37
	Star-gazing	41
	Going to school	46
	Employment opportunities without academic qualifications	48

Chapter 4	**Religion – A Tudor Minefield**	53
	The way things were before	53
	Don't speak out about what monarchs are doing	57
	A Bible in English	60
	Changing times	65
Chapter 5	**Food and Health**	70
	What is new on the Tudor menu?	74
	Behave yourself at table	75
	Caring for the family	78
	New diseases	83
	Remedies	85
Chapter 6	**The Problems of Fashion**	87
	Women's dress	87
	Accessories	91
	The ruff – the epitome of Elizabethan fashion	94
	Men's dress	96
	Footwear	99
	Acts of Apparel	100
Chapter 7	**Home and Family**	105
	Henry VIII – a much-married monarch	108
	Childbirth – 'To be or not to be?'	113
	Royal husbands and wannabes	117
Chapter 8	**Surviving at the Royal Court**	123
	Surviving fickle fortune	123
	Surviving the plague	125

		Secret agents and assassins	127
		A scapegoat?	134
		A playwright, an atheist and a spy	136
Chapter 9	**Travel**		141
	Travel by road		141
	All at sea		145
	The American dream		148
	Exploring Europe		151
Chapter 10	**Leisure Time**		159
	Writing for money		159
	Playing games		166
	Football – England's not-so-beautiful game		174
	Music		176
	Conclusion		178

Notes 179
List of Illustrations 184
Suggested Further Reading 188
Acknowledgements 189
Index 190

Chapter 1

An Introduction to How to Survive in Tudor England

Have you ever read H.G. Wells's novel, *The Time Machine* or watched the BBC's *Doctor Who*, travelling in the TARDIS or 'Time-And-Relative-Dimensions-In-Space' invention? Wouldn't it be marvellous if we really could travel back in history – or even forward to the future? Perhaps, one day that will be possible and all those mysteries of the past can be solved. I have no idea what the future will look like but I know a little bit about our history, so this book is intended as a handy guide – and a cautionary tale – for anyone planning a trip back in time to observe, first-hand, life in England during the reigns of the Tudor monarchs.

England's history is very long and, for convenience, is often chopped into distinct chunks, mainly for the benefit of the school curriculum, the university prospectus, historical timelines and perhaps historians themselves. The centuries before the year ad 1485 [or ce, if you prefer] are usually termed 'medieval' or the 'Middle Ages', although historians are often vague about whether to include the Anglo-Saxon period in these catch-all terms. Or should the 'medieval' period begin when William the Conqueror invaded England and defeated the last Anglo-Saxon king, Harold II, at the battle of Hastings in 1066? A dramatic battle seems to be as good a starting point as any for a new historical era.

After the 'medieval' era, we have the Tudors, including the famous Henry VIII and his six wives and the glories and the swashbuckling excitement of Elizabeth I's reign. The Tudors also see the opening of the 'early modern era', the subsequent term applied to our history up until Queen Victoria took the throne in 1837. With the incredible number of books, films and TV docu-dramas, school projects and PhD theses about the Tudors, you may be surprised to hear that the Tudors ruled England for only 118 years, compared to the previous Plantagenets who were Kings of England from December 1154 to August 1485 – that's 331 years! Which raises two important questions: first, why all the fuss about the Tudors? And second, what happened in August 1485 to change our history from 'medieval' to 'early modern'? If I may, I'll deal with the second question first because the answer to the other question is going to fill the rest of this book.

What happened to the Plantagenets in August 1485?

Briefly, in August 1485, history repeated itself. Just as in 1066, an invader came from France, claiming he had a better right to the English Crown than the current wearer. The invader faced the King of England across the battlefield and, more by luck than anything else, killed the king and proclaimed himself the rightful king by conquest in the former monarch's place. On this occasion, the invader was Henry Tudor; the King of England was Richard III and the decisive conflict was the battle of Bosworth, which took place on 22 August 1485.

Unlike 1066, the king's opponent was a Welshman, not a Norman, although both had sailed from France. Also, the battle of Hastings lasted all day until King Harold was finally slain, whereas the battle of Bosworth was all over well before lunchtime, King Richard having been cut down as he made a courageous but reckless charge against the enemy. Richard was the last Plantagenet King of England and the last English monarch to die in battle. Therefore, once again, a battle marks the end of a historical era – the 'medieval' period.

But the ordinary man or woman in the street would hardly have noticed anything different. They didn't get up on the 23 August and think 'Oh, isn't it exciting, the early modern Tudor period has begun'. Except for the name of the king – when they got to hear of it – nothing very much changed. However, Henry Tudor does appear to have brought two new things along with his army from France: a fashion for square-toed footwear, as opposed to the long pointed-toe style that was popular with Richard III's subjects, and a previously unknown disease which acquired the name 'sweating sickness'. A number of Tudor celebrities die of this ailment so it gets quite a lot of publicity – see Chapter 5.

Setting the Scene

After Henry Tudor was victorious at Bosworth and proclaimed himself king, he took the unprecedented step of dating his reign as having begun the day *before* the battle. It might not sound like much to add an extra day to your time upon the throne, but it was actually a very risky thing to do and Henry's counsellors strenuously advised him not to. But Henry was determined. By insisting he was already King of England before the battle even began, Richard III and all his loyal supporters could be accused of treason on a technicality, having taken up arms against the 'true and rightful' king.

Of course it was all a fiction, but Henry forced his first Parliament to confirm this in a legal act making any survivors on Richard's side vulnerable. Henry could put them under attainder which meant their lands, property and titles were confiscated and their heirs couldn't inherit anything. If he wished, the new king could have them tried and executed for treason. His advisors pointed out that any future invader intent on taking Henry's place, should he succeed, might well do the same to the Tudor supporters. This possibility could deter Henry's subjects from standing by him in battle. Henry chose to ignore the warning – and he had his reasons.

The royal coffers were depleted. Richard's need to raise an army to face the Tudor and his insistence on repaying any debts owed by the Crown had emptied the treasury. Rather than executing too many of

Richard's loyal men, Henry decided to pardon most of them – for an exorbitant sum – and to give back at least some of their properties in return for payment of huge fines. All money made went into Henry's piggy bank. Any unreturned titles and lands could either be bestowed as rewards to Henry's supporters, or sold to help further refill the coffers. Henry Tudor's interest in money was such that he is the only English monarch to bequeath a fortune to his successor.

Therefore, since the first Tudor reign now begins on 21 August 1485, officially, that means King Richard III was alive for just one day of Henry's kingship and our timeline permits us to speak to Richard. If you have heard anything about the last Plantagenet, apart from the discovery of his skeleton in a Leicester car park in 2012, it's probably about the controversy of the missing Princes in the Tower. The princes were Richard's nephews, the sons of his elder brother King Edward IV, but their mother's marriage to Edward was found to be dubious, so the young boys and their sisters were declared illegitimate and couldn't inherit the throne. Richard was crowned instead, but a short while after his coronation the boys disappeared. Nobody knows for certain what happened to them, although rumours ran, and mystery still surrounds their fate today. Henry Tudor wanted answers but never got them. However, we can ask King Richard himself.

Richard III, 1483–85.

An Introduction to How to Survive in Tudor England

It is the evening of 21 August and the royal army is encamped a few miles from the village of Market Bosworth in Leicestershire. King Richard has just finished holding council with his battle captains, working out the tactics for tomorrow. His priest is waiting to hear the king's confession – just in case the worst happens – but we have been granted a brief audience.

'Well, my good man, you know I always try to give my loyal subjects a chance to speak to me. My chamberlain tells me you have a most urgent question to ask, although I cannot think of any matter so important that it may not wait until after the battle tomorrow. But ask it anyway.'

'Thank you, your Grace. My lord, this is a most delicate question but my readers want to know what has happened to your nephews: the little Princes in the Tower.'

'Oh, not that old chestnut again. How tiresome, but I suppose my people deserve the truth. I would say look to my other nephews and nieces. Have I not cared for them? Honoured and respected them all? If you fear I destroyed Edward's sons because they have a better right to the crown than I do, see young Warwick, my brother Clarence's lad. He too might be said to have a stronger claim than I but for his father's attainder, (which was imposed by Edward, not me). England always has need of a strong king. For an untried child to rule is a grave risk in these perilous times. When the peers of the realm and the churchmen begged me to accept the crown, I was reluctant but realised it was my duty to do so, to spare England another civil war. Yet it has brought me nothing but heartache and a great burden of trouble.'

'Yes, sire. You have our condolences on the death of your only son and heir last year and the recent loss of your queen.'

'Two terrible sorrows I must bear...'

'But where are King Edward's sons? Please tell us before it's too late.'

'Too late? You speak as though you expect me to lose the forthcoming battle against the wretched Tudor upstart. This is treasonous talk. Are you a Tudor spy? No doubt he wants to know where the boys can be found so he can slay them. Why do you suppose I have gone to so much effort to keep them safe and their whereabouts a secret? So they do not fall into Tudor's hands. Tomorrow, when the Welshman lies dead upon the field, I shall reveal all because the danger will be past. Now go. My confessor is ready and even kings should not keep God waiting.'

'Thank you for your time, sire. I would wish you good luck for the battle but…'

'Get out before I have you arrested as a Tudor agent!'[1]

A royal shoe comes flying after me as I leave the king's tent, hastily. My apologies to readers – we aren't much wiser concerning the fate of those princes. Henry VII never solves the mystery either.

Now Richard III is no more and the Tudor era really begins. If you know anything about the history of sixteenth-century England, you may realise you are going to have to navigate the dangerous waters of the Reformation, royal marriages, religious persecution and Elizabethan intrigue. This book is a guide to blending into Tudor society at a time of great and rapid change: what to wear, what to eat and how to behave in order to avoid catching the eye of kings, queens, spies and executioners.

But Tudor England also has its lighter moments. You may enjoy staged dramas, new types of music, poetry and plays, or even circumnavigate the globe, if you are in search of adventure. Science is advancing; language is changing but this must-have guide will assist you in staying safe while having a good time and – most important of all – keeping your head.

An Introduction to How to Survive in Tudor England

A brief overview of Tudor history

Whatever the rights and wrongs of their accession to the throne, the Tudors are the newcomers among the royal houses of Europe and an unknown quantity. They have to earn their reputation but nobody trusts them and, as you'll come to realise, they don't trust anyone else in return. The Tudors are suspicious of everybody and their paranoia colours every aspect of their rule.

As a new arrival in Tudor England yourself, you present a danger to a king who is well aware of his own vulnerability, so you need to keep a low profile. However, your speech will mark you out as a 'foreigner'.

Early Tudor English is very different to our language and you'll probably find it hard to understand at first. Even if you make a detailed study of William Shakespeare's works before you go, don't forget that he is believed to have invented many new words and phrases that probably won't be around in the year 1500, almost a century before he began writing his plays.

You might do better to read Thomas Malory's *Morte d'Arthur*, the stories of King Arthur and the Knights of the Round Table, first published by William Caxton in 1485. This text is probably closer to what is spoken by the early Tudor citizens. Henry VII most likely read the book and was aware how much his people admired the legendary king because he chose to name his first-born son and heir Arthur.

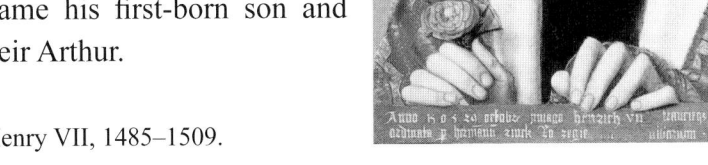

Henry VII, 1485–1509.

However, even Shakespeare was still using old fashioned words such as 'wot', meaning 'know'. 'I wot you well' and 'it's not what you wot but who you wot', as they say – confusing, eh?

Understanding and learning the language is a good start but a first impression is probably even more important. You have to dress the part and in order to do that you need to decide whether you're a yeoman or a serving maid; a merchant or a starch-maker, a nobleman or a lady-in-waiting to the queen. For now, I suggest you keep yourself among those of lesser status until you learn how to manage the risks of promotion to the higher ranks. I cannot over stress the fact that Tudor England is a dangerous place. Clothing for ordinary folk doesn't change dramatically from medieval to Tudor. Modest gowns for both men and women are still the safest option. Shoes and women's headwear are the simplest forms of keeping up with fashion. We've already heard that pointed, or piked, shoes go out with the Plantagenets, replaced by square toes, although the Elizabethans revert to more elegant, pointed footwear. For women, caps of various styles go in and out of fashion but the medieval wimple and veil disappear. Henry VII's mother, Lady Margaret Beaufort, wears the English gabled hood.

At least under Henry VII religious belief is still quite straightforward. Everyone is Roman Catholic and, as yet, there isn't much alternative. The first Tudor monarch executed one earl, one baron, five knights,

Did You Know?

William Shakespeare invented over 1,700 new words, often by changing nouns into verbs – such as blanket, elbow, eyeball and undress (originally meaning a dishevelled state) – adapting verbs into nouns – such as assassination and critic – and making adjectives by connecting words never used together before – such as cold-blooded. But how did medieval folk manage without 'undress' and 'gossip' as verbs; the adjectives 'lonely' and 'obscene' and the noun 'excitement'?

An Introduction to How to Survive in Tudor England

Lady Margaret Beaufort, Henry Tudor's mother.

two leading rebels, two pretenders to the throne and one Lollard (religious) heretic, apart from an assortment of criminals in general, of course. On the subject of religion, things get really DANGEROUS in the reign of Henry VIII.

Now he is a monarch who appears to want to make things as awkward as possible for everyone, whether they're the lowliest beggar or the Pope himself, and the king's closest friends and relatives are often the most at risk. Henry VIII executed two queens, one duke, one marquis, three earls, one countess, one viscount, three barons, two lord chancellors, six knights, seven courtiers, a selection of abbots and priors, one bishop, dozens of monks and nuns, numerous assorted rebels, one heretic, one witch and two unpopular tax-collectors (Richard Empson and Edmund Dudley), along with thousands of unnamed victims. According to the contemporary chronicler Ralph Holinshed, Henry VIII disposed of an incredible 72,000 people during his thirty-eight years on the throne.

Edward VI only reigned for three and a half years but executed a duke and a baron, both of whom were his mother's brothers, and numerous rebels. His half-sister, Mary Tudor, ruled for less than five and a half years but her catalogue of executions is impressive, leading to her gory nickname of Bloody Mary – it's not just a cocktail! Mary accounted for one queen and her consort, two dukes, five knights, one archbishop, three bishops and a writer of the Bible in English, along with hundreds of ordinary folk known as 'Protestant martyrs', who wanted to remain Protestant when Mary tried to return England to Catholicism.

Elizabeth I reigned for forty-five years, so had far more time to make enemies requiring due punishment. She was fairly restrained, however, executing one queen, one duke, two earls, six knights, three Catholic priests (known as 'Catholic martyrs') and nine plotters, two would-be assassins, including a royal physician, and various other miscreants.

N.B. These lists are a guide, by no means exhaustive, but you get the idea.

Henry VII was a paranoid miser; Henry VIII was a megalomaniac who, nevertheless, seems to have suffered with an inferiority complex when comparing himself to other European monarchs. I suppose he was only second generation royalty on his father's side, whereas the French kings of the house of Valois had ruled since 1328 and the

Henry VIII, 1509–47.

> **Did You Know?**
>
> If a film or book about any monarch before 1519 has them addressed as 'majesty', it's just plain wrong.

Habsburgs had been kings and emperors since 1273. In 1500, Charles Habsburg had become the Holy Roman Emperor as Charles V – he was also Katherine of Aragon's nephew. An emperor outranks a king, so this must have been galling for Henry VIII. Charles was also keen on self-promotion and, in 1519, decided he deserved a superior form of address: from now on, he must be referred to as 'your Majesty'. This was a new title. But both Henry and Francis I of France, not to be outdone, swiftly commanded that they too must be addressed as 'majesty'.

Henry went even further in 1533 when, having realised the Pope wasn't going to grant him a divorce from Katherine of Aragon so he could marry Anne Boleyn, and Charles V was openly supporting his Aunt Katherine, he caused England to break away from the Roman Catholic Church. Thomas Cromwell drew up a carefully worded Act of Parliament which forbade any future appeals to be made to the Pope and also raised King Henry's status by claiming:

> This realm of England is an Empire and so hath been accepted in the world, governed by one Supreme Head and King having the dignity and royal estate of the Imperial Crown of the same.

You have to wonder who 'in the world' had accepted England as an empire when Calais was her only overseas possession at the time. But upgrading a kingdom to an empire made Henry an emperor in all but name and the equal of his nemesis, Charles V.

Henry VIII's 'Jewel', his son Edward VI, though only 9 years old when he succeeded his father in 1547 was, nevertheless, a keen and zealous supporter of the new Protestant religion and the now independent Church of England, of which he was head. Being young, he required adult supervision to assist him to rule. Henry VIII had intended the lad to have a regency council to do this but his powerful uncle, Edward Seymour, Duke of Somerset, took charge, making himself Edward's Lord Protector – king in all but name. But there were various rebellions – surprisingly, one in Devon and Cornwall was against having to use the new Prayer Book which was written in English not Latin – and the threat of a French invasion and so much unrest was blamed on Seymour.

John Dudley, the eldest son of Edmund Dudley, the unpopular tax-gatherer executed by Henry VIII, now Earl of Warwick, had some success in putting down the revolts and caused Seymour's downfall. You won't be surprised to hear that Seymour was arrested and – you guessed it – lost his head. Warwick promoted himself to Duke of Northumberland and he and young King Edward set to work, making England ever more Protestant in its worship. All Catholic imagery:

stained-glass windows, wall paintings of religious subjects, images of saints and the Virgin Mary, crucifixes and rosaries were destroyed. High Altars were reckoned to remove God from close contact with the congregation, so rood screens were demolished and the altar became an ordinary table where humble folk could take communion along with the vicar.

All this religious reform seemed to be going well when the young king fell seriously ill. Edward's closest heir was his elder half-sister Mary, daughter of Katherine of Aragon. Mary was a

Edward VI, 1547–53.

devout Catholic and neither the young king nor Dudley could bear the idea that all their work would be undone if she became queen.

Both Mary and Edward's other half-sister, Elizabeth, daughter of Anne Boleyn, had been declared bastards by their father, Henry VIII, so couldn't legally inherit the throne. Edward and Dudley would have preferred Elizabeth to become queen because she, like Edward, had been raised and educated as a Protestant. It was possible to have Parliament pass an act, making Elizabeth legitimate – it had been done before to legitimise Henry VII's Beaufort ancestors – but would automatically make Mary legitimate as well. So this wasn't an option.

Instead, Dudley hastily arranged for his youngest son, Guildford (the only one not already wed), to marry a young lass, Lady Jane Grey. She and the king were the same age and their marriage had been suggested earlier, when Edward was still in good health. Jane was the perfect Protestant and King Edward's *legitimate* cousin, granddaughter of Henry VIII's sister, Mary, Duchess of Suffolk. Dudley persuaded the dying king to sign a new Act of Succession, naming Jane as his heir. When Edward died on 6 July 1553, Jane became Queen of England with Guildford Dudley as her consort. The Dudley family had risen from tax-gatherers to king-in-all-but-name, since it was thought at the time that no woman could rule without a man to tell her what to do.

Sadly for Queen Jane, her reign lasted, famously, for just nine days. The people weren't bothered about Mary being legitimate or not. They regarded her as the rightful heir. The fact that she

Did You Know?

England had never had a queen regnant before – that is a queen ruling in her own right, rather than a queen consort, the wife of a king. But at this point in Tudor history ALL the possible heirs were female! England was going to have a woman on the throne, one way or another, like it or not.

Lady Jane Grey, queen for nine days in July 1553.

was an ardent Catholic appealed to many who weren't nearly so keen on Protestantism with its plain glass, white-washed walls and the abolition of saints. That the Catholic church services were in Latin – a language few ordinary folk could understand – was just the way it should be because Latin was God's language, or so it was believed. Mary became queen on a tidal wave of popular support, but it didn't last.

Mary wasn't so young and England needed an heir urgently, so her priority was to get married and get pregnant as soon as possible. Just a year after her succession, Mary wed her cousin Philip, son of Charles V, the Holy Roman Emperor (remember him?), heir to the throne of Spain. At the time, the English hated anything Spanish almost as much as they loathed anything French. It was a bad move on Mary's part. Whereas she was delighted to have a husband who was as keen to restore England to the Catholic faith as she was, her subjects hated the idea of being ruled by a detested Spaniard and the possibility of being dragged into Spanish politics and expensive foreign wars. There was a rebellion raised to show how deeply Philip was resented. As a result, heads rolled, of course, including the Duke of Northumberland's, that of his son, Guildford Dudley, and inevitably, poor Jane Grey's, though Mary was rumoured to be reluctant to sign the death warrant for Jane's execution.

An Introduction to How to Survive in Tudor England

Mary I, aka 'Bloody Mary', 1553–58.

Elizabeth, Mary's half-sister, suspected of being behind the rebellion, was imprisoned in the Tower of London, fearing she would be next in line for the headsman's block. She vehemently stated that she was innocent, knowing nothing of the uprising. Mary let her live. Meanwhile, the queen was busy, restoring the Catholic faith in England. The list of Protestant martyrs burned at the stake for refusing to return to Catholicism included three bishops. Mary's popularity waned and the desired heir was never born. In November 1558, Mary died and was succeeded by Elizabeth. It was 'all-change' again for religion: Catholics out; Protestants in once more.

Mary's widower, Philip, now King Philip II of Spain, thought he might be able to keep England loyal to the Pope if he married the new Queen Elizabeth. She was having none of it. Elizabeth knew better than to upset her subjects. However, she too was expected to marry and produce an heir to continue the Tudor dynasty. This was a tricky situation. If she took a foreign husband of suitable rank, England could become embroiled in European politics, as Philip had tried to do. Any husband had to be Protestant in order to avoid more religious upheavals but there were few Protestant suitors to choose from. Perhaps an English husband was the answer? But whoever she chose from among her noblemen, his fellow peers would resent his rise to power and probably rebel. In the end, although it took her subjects decades to realise the fact, Elizabeth took the unprecedented

Elizabeth I, 1558–1603.

and wisest option: she didn't marry anybody. She remained the Virgin Queen and kept both the royalty of Europe and her people guessing – will she; won't she? – but it must have been a lonely life.

I think the man who came closest to marrying her (and may have been her lover) was Robert Dudley, Earl of Leicester. He was another son of the Duke of Northumberland and had narrowly escaped execution, along with his father, his younger brother Guildford and sister-in-law, Queen Jane. Robert had spent time imprisoned in the Tower of London, just like Elizabeth. Both had lost a parent to the executioner. They were close in age, education and religious beliefs. The trouble was that Robert already had a wife, Amy. When Amy died in a fall down the stairs, it all seemed a bit too convenient to be an accident. The queen couldn't possibly marry a murder suspect, even though nothing was ever proven. When the rumours subsided, Robert returned as Elizabeth's favourite but the marriage never happened.

A few foreign suitors were entertained, including the brother of the King of France, but I think they knew their chances were slim, especially with Robert still at court. When Robert died in 1588, Elizabeth was heartbroken and it was too late anyway to take a husband and produce an heir because she was now 55 years old. England was reconciled to the fact that the Tudor dynasty would come to an end when the queen died. But who could possibly take her place? Everyone held their breath when, in March 1603, after forty-five years on the throne and having proved a woman was quite capable of ruling alone, it became clear that Good Queen Bess, the Virgin Queen, Gloriana, was dying. The Tudor period of England's history was over.

So now you have a brief overview of the dynamic and troubled Tudor age. If I haven't put you off and you still intend to time-travel to see for yourself what life was like back then, the following chapters may help you to survive that perilous era without following in the footsteps of those unfortunate queens, nobles, churchmen and thousands of ordinary folk who met their ends far sooner than they should have done.

Chapter 2

Social Structure

As with so many societies across the world in our own times, in Tudor England there is a wide chasm dividing the rich and the poor. This had been true in medieval times – no one could mistake the gap between the earl and the serfs who worked his land – but at least there was employment for everyone and food and shelter available for all. Unfortunately, this situation is beginning to change by the Tudor era. The first problem is something called 'enclosures'.

Enclosures refer to the fencing off or hedging of large fields to 'enclose' huge numbers of sheep and keep them from wandering off. Well-to-do yeomen – the better-off farmers of the day – buy up the smaller holdings of their poorer neighbours and turn the land into one big sheep farm. Sheep can be cared for by just a couple of shepherds with a bit of extra help at lambing and shearing time, so the wages bill for the yeoman is small but the profits from selling the wool can be huge. It's a get-rich-quick recipe and landowners across England see the benefits as the country yeomen become wealthy gentlemen-farmers. Which is excellent news for some but what about the poorer neighbours whose land now grows nothing but grass for the sheep?

Being poor

Unless the poor neighbour gets employment as a shepherd, he could be jobless, unable to grow his own food and without money to pay the rent or feed and clothe his family. What can he do but go looking for work elsewhere? The trouble is there are thousands just like him and things get worse. With far less food being grown for human consumption, prices rise dramatically, just for a loaf of bread or a single egg. This is problem number two: inflation. But at least the poor can still drop by the local abbey or priory and claim 'dole', which is usually bread and ale enough to keep you going until tomorrow. These religious houses occasionally give out alms in the form of second-hand clothing or old blankets which can save the homeless family from dying of cold. They also provide care for the sick and infirm, as well as schooling and education. Monasteries and nunneries are the welfare system of the day, which brings us to problem number three: the Dissolution.

Mainly for personal reasons – see Chapter 4 – King Henry VIII decides to close all the religious houses in England. This is known as the Dissolution and is his get-rich-quick recipe as well as a metaphorical poke in the eye for the Pope in Rome – great for Henry but a disaster for the poor, the homeless and the unemployed who are increasing in number daily. Suddenly, there is no welfare to be had except from charitable individuals and the parish church, but these usually confine their donations to local folk in trouble, not those who have walked miles in search of work.

Inevitably, many of these unemployed and homeless people turn to begging in an attempt to feed their families, but it's all too easy to slip into a life of crime. The disabled and elderly who cannot work are

FACTS

There are three important causes of poverty in Tudor England:

1. Enclosures – turning crop growing land into sheep farms causing unemployment and reduced food production.
2. Inflation – higher prices for basic foodstuffs because fewer crops are grown.
3. The Dissolution – the closure of the monasteries and nunneries means there are no hospitals, no care for the poor, needy and homeless.

seen as deserving Christian charity, so they're granted licences to beg by the authorities. But so-called 'sturdy' beggars and vagabonds who are quite capable of working for a living, if only they can find a job, are regarded as either too lazy to do a hand's turn or else they must be up to no good, threatening honest citizens, so no licences are granted to them. For those who have no skills to earn a living and no licence to plead for alms, there is only one alternative to starvation: theft.

In 1531, Henry VIII's answer to this problem is to introduce more stringent punishments: death for stealing the most trivial items. His chancellor, Sir Thomas More, is less than impressed:

> This punishment of thieves passes the limits of Justice … it is too extreme and cruel a punishment for theft and yet not sufficient to refrain and withhold men from theft. For simple theft is not so great an offence that it ought to be punished with death. Neither is there any punishment so horrible that it can keep them from stealing which have no other craft whereby to get their living … no man should be driven to this extreme necessity, first to steal and then to die.

With the closure of the monasteries, priories and friaries by Henry VIII in the late 1530s, homeless monks, nuns and their lay servants swell the numbers of unemployed, often with no skills or trade to earn their living any other way. Some of the better educated monks are taken on as tutors to the children of the wealthy but, at the other extreme, some poor nuns turn to prostitution to avoid starvation.

Top Tip

For many poor folk, a life of petty crime is the only answer but the penalty for stealing an egg – which had been a one shilling (12d) fine (steep enough if you are penniless) – is now death! You have been warned.

Clearly, the majority of those without a job are honest folk with no intention of turning to crime to feed, clothe and provide shelter for themselves and their families. So what are their alternative means of support? The sad answer is: very little.

Dealing with the poor

Authorities, from the monarch to the local parish, have no method of dealing with the jobless except to move them somewhere else, into some other authority's jurisdiction. 'Every beggar suitable to work shall resort to the Hundred [a local community of roughly one hundred households] where he last dwelled, is best known, or was born and there [to] remain.' This hardly helps anyone. People move away from their impoverished parishes in the first place, hoping to find employment in some more affluent town. Having failed to get a job – and this is never easy because each town has its own guild system which ensures those who are locally trained are employed in preference to outsiders – they are now sent back to the same poor parish where they were unable to make a living before. The poorer the parish, the more beggars and vagrants it is likely to be expected to support and, of course, it can't.

In 1535, with the Dissolution of the Monasteries in full swing, it's suggested that a law should be passed to provide for the poor, using public funds raised by a tax on income and capital. But such a tax is never going to be popular with the wealthy men (it's men only) sitting in Parliament, so the law never passes. Instead, another law is introduced permitting vagrants, beggars and vagabonds to be whipped – as if that will help.

Tudor London, as throughout its long history, always attracts people hoping to improve their lives. The city has crowds of poor folk to deal with and no way of organising this. The famous St Bartholomew's Hospital – still there in the twenty-first century – had been run by monks for centuries, giving aid to the sick and

St Bartholomew the Great's Church (interior), Smithfield, London.

dying. Now, with the monasteries closed, the hospital is no longer available. Even King Henry realises St Bart's, as it's known, had served a vital function and he allows it to reopen in 1544, run by lay persons, not monks, but it's to be paid for by the citizens of London, supposedly voluntarily. At first, money for the staff's wages, the upkeep of the buildings and the provisions required to care for the patients is raised from the Sunday collections taken in church, but this is never enough. The citizens themselves are

Did You Know?

One dangerous employment opportunity is that of salvage diver. Jacques Francis from Mauritius is paid to recover the valuable cannons from Henry VIII's flagship, *Mary Rose,* after she sank off the Isle of Wight in 1545, and manages to raise a few by free-diving.

having a hard time with soaring food prices and must tighten their belts, so they have little spare cash to give to charity.

In 1547, the first compulsory 'Poor Rate' is introduced to pay for St Bart's and, in 1552 this is extended by young Edward VI to pay for the reopening of St Thomas's Hospital across the River Thames, in Southwark. But still London is overwhelmed by the number of fit, able people who wander its streets in search of work, resorting to petty crime to survive. In 1555, King Edward donates his palace at Bridewell, just outside the city, as the first House of Correction. As the name suggests, it's more like a prison than a place of relief and assistance but at least the poor can find shelter there, a bed and food provided, however miserable the quality. In exchange, they must work at such tasks as featherbed making, stitching caps and wire-drawing.

Sturdy rogues and con-artists

You won't be surprised to hear that the more imaginative poor folk (and a few of the not so poor) find some intriguing ways of avoiding places like Bridewell, getting their hands on money without actually stealing it – not too obviously, at least. We know about their devious methods because Thomas Harman, a Kentish gentleman, comes across so many of these 'sturdy rogues' as he calls them in the course of his work as a magistrate. In 1567 he compiles 'a dictionary of beggary' as a warning against the various kinds of con-artists, all out to 'gull' the innocent.

One of the most successful and persistent offenders caught by Harman is Nicholas Jennings, aka Nicholas Blunt, an Elizabethan con-man with a considerable repertoire of methods. He has made so much money by nefarious means that he lives in a nice house across the Thames in Newington but continues in his criminal ways until the law gets him in the end. He has already been whipped through the busy London streets and is now sitting in the pillory in Cheapside, to

The front cover of Thomas Harman's pamphlet about beggars and con-men, 1567.

be laughed at and humiliated, pelted with dung, mud and rotten veg. Let's ask him about his crimes:

> 'Good afternoon, Jennings – although I suppose it's not such a good afternoon for you, is it? Since you're stuck here in the pillory with nothing better to do, would you mind telling our readers about the different types of con-tricks you've used to make a living?'
>
> 'Go away.'
>
> 'Oh, I thought you'd like to boast about how clever you are. I did hear that you're one of the best counterfeit-cranks and upright-men in London.'
>
> 'Not "one of". I'm *the* best and a brilliant clapper-dudgeon too. I know every trick there is.'
>
> 'Can you explain what you do?'

24

'Well, see, a counterfeit-crank pretends to suffer the falling-sickness – epilepsy the physicians call it. I put a little soap on my tongue – tastes horrible but I'm willing to suffer for my art – then I fall down, kicking and jerking and seeming to foam at the mouth. I'm very convincing. People feel sorry for me and throw money, the fools. It works the same when I play the clapper-dudgeon with fake sores, boils and bleeding wounds, all cunningly made with butchers' offal and a hidden pig's bladder full of chicken blood.'

'What about being an upright-man? Tell us about that.'

'An upright-man doesn't commit crimes himself but organises other thieves and beggars, taking a share of their profits having taught them the best ways to ply their various trades. My hookers earn a good living.'

'You mean "women of the night"?'

'No. Don't be stupid. Hookers visit houses and shops during daylight, innocently asking the directions to somewhere or other, or begging a cup of water. All the while, they're looking out for clothing or goods worth stealing. Knowing exactly what to take and where it is, they return after dark and "hook" the goods – all very efficient.'

'What other tricks do you use, Jennings?'

'I've been a whipjack, playing a sailor whose ship was wrecked and he barely survived. That always earns sympathy. And a ring-faller – that's a good one. I drop a cheap brass ring on the ground just as my chosen fool comes along. I tell him I've lost a valuable gold ring that I was going to sell and if he helps me find it, I'll share the profits. We recover the ring and do a friendly deal. I give it to him in exchange for his payment to me of half its value because he knows a jeweller who'll give him a good price. I'm reluctant to part with it, of course, but he insists. When he sells the ring, the fool learns it's worthless. I've also claimed to be the victim of a garrotting, though I've never committed that crime myself.'

'You pretend to be strangled?'

'No. Is that what you think garrotting means? It's a violent street robbery. I don't like hurting people, only their purses. Hey! Don't go yet. Wipe this stinking muck off my face for me. It's the least you can do in exchange for this valuable lesson.'

'Farewell, Jennings. Enjoy your afternoon.'[1]

Having heard about some of these con-tricks from Nicholas Jennings you'll know what to look out for on the streets. Further Vagabond and Poor Acts are introduced in the reigns of Mary I and Elizabeth I but they don't help very much. Then, in 1597, things get worse when a series of crop failures, rapid inflation and economic decline add to the number on the breadline, while charitable donations fall away to almost nothing.

Going abroad

However, a new way of moving the poor around, out of sight elsewhere, begins in the 1580s. Ireland needs fit, healthy workers to colonise her empty land. George Peckham thinks 'the great numbers which live in such penury and want... could serve there one year for meat, drink and apparel only, without wages... to amend their estates'. Richard Hakluyt has an even better idea, to ship them off to the New World across the Atlantic. And not only the poor and unemployed can take up this 'indentured [on a contract] service'; why not empty England's prisons and send the inmates to America? By 1619, into the Stuart period, this system is populating Virginia with poor folk, hoping to make a new life.

So if you fancy foreign travel, this might be an option. Passports aren't required but don't expect a first class cabin. You'll probably have to 'work your passage' to pay for the voyage, share your

Social Structure

> 📌 **Top Tip**
>
> No doubt, you will realise by now that travelling back to Tudor times and being one of the poor is probably not the best option. It would be better to be wealthier: a gentleman or his lady at the very least.

accommodation – and maybe even your hammock – with your unwashed fellows and there'll be no lazing on the beach when you arrive. This isn't the easy alternative.

Being a gentleman or lady

In my opinion, being a member of the up-and-coming gentlemanly class, so long as you're not too ambitious, is probably the safest choice in Tudor England. You are not scratching a living in poverty but neither are you so rich and powerful that you attract the notice of your monarch. New Tudor houses are becoming far more comfortable, if you can afford one, with fancy chimneys, glass windows and wood panelling to keep out the draughts. The shared living accommodation

Ightham Mote, Kent.

of medieval times is out of fashion and the modern family likes to eat and sleep more privately.

Richard Clement is a gentleman, probably born in 1482. Before 1509, he had married a wealthy widow, Anne Whittlebury of Northampton, so the couple are comfortably off. He buys a medieval manor house in Kent, known as Ightham Mote, in 1521 for £400. He decides that Ightham Mote is far too out-of-date for a fashionable gentleman so he begins an expensive rebuilding scheme on his new home. He adds a crenellated gatehouse tower to impress his visitors as they arrive. He has large stained-glass windows put into the original medieval great hall, making it much brighter, and has his coat-of-arms, along with the king's and the pomegranate badge of Katherine of Aragon, Henry VIII's first wife, displayed in the coloured glass. Tudor heraldry is everywhere. He builds a magnificent guest suite in a new upper storey with grand chambers, a convenient privy and the latest in fine living – a long gallery, so guests can take indoor walks in wet weather. You have to wonder if Clement was hoping for a royal visit. None is recorded but he does receive an invitation to Anne Boleyn's coronation at Westminster Abbey in 1533.

In 1528, his first wife dies and now he is a knight, Sir Richard Clement, his second wife can be a little higher up the social scale. In 1530, he marries Lady Anne, the widow of John, Lord Grey, hoping for more court connections. He dies in his comfortable bedchamber at Ightham Mote in 1538, aged 56, and is buried in the village church beside his first wife with a fine brass monument to mark his last resting

Did You Know?

At Clement's house of Ightham Mote there is some unusual wood panelling, known as 'Biblefold'. Its design is supposed to be unique to Cardinal Wolsey's private closet at Hampton Court. Clement was a bit of a 'wheeler-dealer' so did he 'acquire' some of this special panelling by less than legal methods; did it 'fall off the back of a Tudor truck'?

place.[2] In his will, he leaves his estate to his widow and although he has no legitimate children by either of his wives, he makes bequests to his 'bastard' daughters. Sir Richard Clement knew how to survive in dangerous Tudor times and 56 is a reasonably good age.

Money

The one thing that a gentleman must have is money – the more the better, although there's nothing wrong with running up a few debts. In fact, debts are almost fashionable, as long as there is an outside chance that you might pay them back eventually.

When he defeats Richard III in 1485, Henry VII is not only determined to refill the empty royal coffers, by whatever means he can – his tax-gatherering methods are notorious – he decides to overhaul the coinage. Firstly, in 1489, he invents the £1 coin, calls it a sovereign and has it minted in gold with his own image on the the obverse – a declaration that the Tudors have arrived, if ever there was one.

The 10 shilling ryal and the 6s 8d angel are both reminted as silver coins, their previously gold counterparts having often been hoarded or melted down into cups, plates and jewellery. Pennies, half-groats (2d)

Henry VII gold Sovereign worth £1, obverse.

and groats are all redesigned and their silver content assured, as well as the new silver shillings by 1504. As a result of his father's financial efforts, Henry VIII inherits vast wealth but he spends the money on lavish living, building fabulous palaces like Nonsuch. He spends a fortune in spectacular displays of conspicuous consumption, such as at the 'Field of the Cloth of Gold', held near Calais in northern France in June 1520 to impress Francis I, King of France. By the 1530s, the king is broke and between 1490 and 1530, prices rise by 70 per cent while wages drop by 50 per cent, that is for those who have any employment at all. And inflation continues, reaching 500 per cent by the end of Queen Elizabeth's reign in 1600.[3] Later in Henry's reign, after his break with Rome in 1533, his coffers are refilled, briefly, by the sale of dissolved monastic estates and ecclesiastical wealth. But his fear of a Catholic invasion attempt against England leads to vast sums being spent on coastal fortifications, warships like the *Mary Rose*, cannon and other armaments as the king's policies concerning the defence of the realm verge upon paranoia.

With his coffers empty, Henry has to choose between economising or increasing the number of coins he has to spend. He decides on the latter, declaring that the sovereign, previously worth £1, is now worth £1 2s 6d without any additional gold added. The silver shilling is reminted with more base metal added and the penny now contains less than half its weight in silver. Old, good quality coins are recalled to the mints and exchanged for the new, less-valuable currency. Since this means the mints themselves are making a considerable profit, in 1544, Henry increases his share of the fees. More mints are set up resulting in an extra £1 million going to the Exchequer in eight years, exceeding the income from taxation by a wide margin. The king must be feeling smug at his ingenuity. But the poor find their few pence can buy even less. The effect on trade is bad because although English exports are now cheaper, the cost of imports soars as foreign merchants refuse to accept English money in payment.

Another factor affecting trade over which Henry has no control but which makes the situation worse is the discovery by the

Spaniards of vast hoards of silver in the Americas. As the precious metal is brought back to Europe by the galleon-load, its value decreases across the trading networks. England's coinage would be reduced in its purchasing power even if it wasn't debased. Overall, in just sixty years, by the time Henry VIII dies in 1547, Henry VII's excellent coinage has become the most adulterated and devalued in Europe, considered worthless in trade, mostly thanks to his spendthrift son.

In the reign of Edward VI, Lord Protector Somerset debases the silver shillings – known as 'testoons' – even more, inventing my favourite coin when I was a child: the sixpence. Then in 1549, England's best source of income, the cloth trade, goes into recession while Somerset runs up huge debts, making war on Scotland and France. As you'll realise, money is a tricky subject in Tudor times.

But one Englishman knows how to handle the financial markets – a genius with money who understands the intrigues of foreign exchange rates – Sir Thomas Gresham. The historian, John Guy, calls this incredibly successful London merchant 'the first true wizard of global finance' and he's very wealthy. While he's here in England, let's take the opportunity to have a chat with Sir Thomas:

> 'Good day, Sir Thomas. I can see you are a man of fashion, wearing all things black.'
>
> 'Black involves using the most expensive dyes, you know. It's the easiest way to demonstrate my wealth and standing to lesser people … like you.'
>
> 'I heard that you buy six new pairs of shoes every year. Isn't that excessive when most people only possess one or two pairs and have them mended, over and over, until they're unwearable?'
>
> 'I buy in bulk. It's cheaper that way and makes sense, financially.'
>
> 'They say you're a wizard with money. Does this ever require any dodgy dealings?'

'Ha, ha. You expect me to give an honest answer? I've smuggled foreign gold coins across borders for the king. That takes skill and daring but don't tell the Emperor Charles V. And I gather intelligence for the queen.'

'You mean you're a spy?'

'If required. But mostly I manage Queen Elizabeth's financial affairs and received a knighthood for my trouble. Her majesty doesn't always like what I do but she realises I know far more about such things than anybody else.'

'In fact, you persuaded the queen that all the coins in the realm should be reminted, reversing the catastrophic mess her father made of England's financial situation.'

'It had to be done. Foreign merchants didn't want to touch our coinage when it wasn't worth the correct value. Now things have greatly improved, thanks to me.'

'Tell us about the Royal Exchange in the heart of the city.'

'That fine building – my vision, constructed at my expense – should be known as Gresham's Exchange but her majesty has other ideas.'

'It is England's first shopping mall. You can be proud of that.'

'Mall? I know not the word.'

'An undercover shopping experience with numerous retail outlets.'

'Yes, I am indeed inordinately proud of it but it's mainly a place for merchants and bankers to do business, out of the weather and at hours regulated by the ringing of the bell.'

'I heard it said that "almost everything a man may imagine by way of costly wares" can be bought at the Exchange.'

Sir Thomas Gresham, c.1565.

'Very true and all is overseen by my badge of the Golden Grasshopper atop the belfry. This is my legacy to London … to England … to the world of finance!'

'Thank you, Sir Thomas. I think we see your point.'[4]

London for the wealthy

According to John Stow, the son of a London tallow-chandler or candle-maker, born in 1525, the city is changing during his lifetime, becoming a prosperous place where stand 'divers fair houses for merchants and other … with small tenements in great number'. The rich and the lesser folk live side by side. In Lothbury, for example, brass- and coppersmiths have their workshops on the north side of the street, making such a din, and yet some posh merchants have their elegant properties on the south

> **❗ Top Tip**
>
> London's streets slope steeply down to the River Thames so take care. In September 1574, during heavy rain, a young man lost his footing when trying to cross Dowgate Hill. He was swept away and drowned even before the watergate at the foot of hill stopped his body falling into the river.[5]

side. Stow says Cheapside, a main east-west thoroughfare across the city that used to be the most important market street in earlier times, is now home to the goldsmiths and money changers. Thomas Gresham lives in Basinghall Street, north of Cheapside and east of Guildhall. This is the classiest part of town where the mercers or cloth-traders have their houses. Blackwell Hall, the centre of the mercers' trade, is rebuilt here in 1588 at the incredible cost of £2,500 – in the twenty-first century that is roughly £2,500,000. Other once-grand establishments are being divided up into smaller tenements for rent.

Stow notes how different crafts are changing their focus of operation, moving about the city. The grocers and apothecaries of Soper Lane have moved to Bucklersbury; the poulterers, after which 'Poultry' was named, are now in Gracechurch Street. But Stow disapproves of some of these changes. For example, Grub Street had been a centre for bowyers and fletchers, making bows and arrows, but now these respectable trades are replaced by 'bowling-alleys and dicing-houses … too much frequented', as Stow complains.

Close by the Tower of London, the former religious house known as the Minories is becoming the centre of gun manufacture and the Crutched Friars is now a glassworks. In Gutter Lane, Nicholas Hilliard trained as a goldsmith but now he works as a painter of miniatures at a house called 'the Maidenhead' in the same street. These are new crafts.

In the next chapter, we can think about what new opportunities you may have in education and employment, including some exciting ventures that may appeal to you.

Chapter 3

Education and Employment Opportunities

Cardinal, Archbishop of York and Lord Chancellor, Thomas Wolsey [*c*.1473–1500] is a great example of what can be achieved by Tudors of humble birth. King Henry VIII prefers his advisors and ministers to be clever men – sorry, it's men only in charge – of ordinary birth. He regards noblemen as untrustworthy and those of ancient lineage also make him feel inferior and he can't have that. Wolsey's father was a lowly butcher so Henry has no problems in promoting him, making certain the man is fully aware that he owes all his success and position to the king who can remove him from office on a whim, if he fails to please. Henry is lazy about matters of state and government, so having an efficient secretary to do the job is the answer.

Wolsey's route to the top was through the church which educated him and saw him attend and graduate at Oxford University. Henry VII noticed him and made him a court chaplain and diplomat. Since he did well, in 1509, Henry VIII promoted him to the King's Council when he ascended the throne.

Now Master of the Rolls and Dean of Lincoln, Wolsey begins to put on airs and graces with a travelling entourage of 200 gentlemen. By 1514, his meteoric rise sees him made Bishop of Lincoln and Archbishop of York shortly afterward. In 1515, Pope Leo X makes him a cardinal and Papal Legate in 1518 which means he outranks the Archbishop of Canterbury as the chief churchman in England.

Hampton Court had been a nice little Thames-side manor house in Henry VII's reign, rented from the local abbey by Sir Giles Daubeney.[1] Wolsey buys the manor outright in 1514 and builds a great, modern, luxurious palace in its place. No wonder Henry VIII

> **Did You Know?**
>
> Thomas Wolsey was a cat lover and his pet is beside him in this modern statue.

looks at Hampton Court with envious eyes. Wolsey, aware that his success couldn't have happened if he hadn't had a good education, sets out to make his home town of Ipswich in Suffolk a seat of learning to rival Oxford and Cambridge. Things don't work out that way in the end but the cardinal understands how young people should be taught. His statue in Ipswich bears the legend: 'Pleasure should mingle with study so that the child may think learning an amusement rather than a toil.' And 'amen' to that.

Thomas Wolsey runs the government of England while his king enjoys a lavish lifestyle. The problem is that the cardinal is brilliant at tax reforms and improving the course of justice, neither of which make him any friends among the most powerful. Wolsey's one big failure causes his downfall – he cannot persuade the Pope to grant the king a divorce from Katherine of Aragon so he can marry Anne Boleyn. Anne

Cardinal Wolsey's statue in Ipswich.

engineers the cardinal's fall from favour in 1530 and no one else speaks up for him. He is swiftly replaced as secretary by a man he has trained himself: Thomas Cromwell, the son of a lowly blacksmith. Meanwhile, the king and Anne Boleyn enjoy the luxuries of Wolsey's Hampton Court. Wolsey isn't tried and executed but only because he dies before that can happen. So beware when you travel back to Tudor times: too much success can be a dangerous thing.

New occupations

If you are educated – and that means knowing Latin, I'm afraid – there are some new jobs available that are less dangerous than being a royal secretary, occupations that either weren't around in medieval times or were hardly known about. Books had existed for a thousand years and more but they had always been hand written by scribes which meant production was slow, and copies were few and expensive. Books to read and educate people were badly needed. Luckily, in Germany in 1440, Johannes Gutenberg invented movable type.

William Caxton brought the first printing press to England in 1476 and set up in business at Westminster. To start with, his customers were kings and nobility wanting high-end books, but after Caxton died in 1492, his assistant – with the marvellously apt name of Wynkyn de Worde – takes over and produces cheap mass-market books that lesser folk can afford to buy. Many of these are educational such as school text books – in Latin – but also self-help books on how to run the household, correct behaviour and dietary and health instruction – in English. It makes learning to read more worthwhile in Tudor times.

If you wish to become a printer, obviously you will have to be able to read, but it gets trickier because the type-face letters are backwards and you need to be able to construct sentences in reverse, from right to left, letter by letter, fitting the tiny pieces of metal into a block called a 'galley'. You have a box or 'case' divided into little pigeon holes, each one holding types of an individual letter or punctuation

A woodcut showing a Tudor printing press, 1568.

mark so it's easy to pick out the next one you need. Letters in the upper pigeon holes are capitals – hence 'upper case' letters. This may take a lot of practice before you become quick and accurate at making up the galleys. The galleys and any woodblock illustrations, all arranged in reverse, are then put into a frame or 'forme', which goes onto the base of the printing press. Then comes the messy bit: inking the words and pictures using leather balls on sticks, one in each hand. Then, with *clean* hands, a blank sheet of paper is laid on top of the inked forme and held in place before the heavy flat platen comes down to press the paper evenly against the forme. This requires muscle power and the lever is a hefty weight so you need to be fit as well as literate to be a printer.

Then you release the platen and take out your beautifully printed page, as in the image above, hopefully with all the words round the right way. If you need more copies of that page just repeat the process

Did You Know?

The Chinese had invented printing some time before AD 200 but using wood blocks in their printing presses. Gutenberg invented individual metal letters and punctuation (type) that could be arranged to spell out anything – backwards!

from the inking-up stage as many times as required. At least you only have to assemble the galley once. With practice, you could print up to 3,600 pages of type in a day.

Another new occupation, though not a job because you won't be paid for your efforts and have nothing to sell – unless you write a book about your work – is that of a scientist. At least, that would be the description in the twenty-first century. The Tudors will refer to you, politely, as a 'natural philosopher', but may call you a magician, an alchemist, an astrologer or a madman behind your back, depending on what sort of science you do and it's possible to combine any or all kinds of subjects together. Doctor John Dee is a brilliant mathematician but also dabbles in astrology and the occult. Queen Elizabeth hires him as her court magician and he is kept busy, studying his astrology charts and calculating the most auspicious days for big events, such as the queen's coronation. Foretelling the future is an important job and you have a definite advantage over any other Tudor astrologer – you already know what's going to happen, at least with the important issues that history has recorded.

For example, when Anne Boleyn becomes pregnant with Henry VIII's child, all the court astrologers confirm that the baby will definitely be a son because that's what the king so desperately wants to hear. But you know it will be a daughter, destined to become Queen Elizabeth I. Do you dare to tell the king the truth? What happened to the astrologers who got it wrong isn't recorded but I doubt they were very popular after that awful mistake.

Perhaps you can be an alchemist – a chemist – if you enjoy laboratory work, although you'll have to learn to blow all your own

Did You Know?

The structure of the printing press is based on those that had been used to press grapes for wine and squeeze olives to extract the olive oil for centuries.

glassware and make your own equipment before you begin. At least you won't have to worry about health and safety issues because nobody bothers about them. Blow up your lab as often as you like; you'll just be reckoned to be another madman, trying to turn base metals into gold and searching for the elusive philosopher's stone.

More useful than alchemy, unless you manage to create gold, is to be an apothecary. This isn't a new job but it can pay well as the Tudor equivalent of a pharmacist and, of course, you know which plants really do have good medicinal effects because of your modern knowledge. What is new about the job are the possibilities of using plants imported from that New World across the Atlantic Ocean. Quinine or cinchona bark is first brought back from Peru by the Spaniards in 1574 and it is used to treat fevers effectively but you know that it can prevent and cure malaria, the dreaded recurrent and agonising fevers the Tudors call the ague. Echinacea or cone flower is used by Native Americans to treat numerous complaints and modern medicine has proved it acts as an excellent boost to the immune system, so you may be able to persuade some enterprising merchant to import the plants from North America.

However, one plant which merchants import with enthusiasm is tobacco. People get rich growing and importing the dried leaves. Today, we know the stuff causes lung cancer but from the sixteenth to the twentieth century, tobacco smoking was believed to be healthy, calming stress and good for chest and respiratory complaints. It's hard to credit now but you will have a hard time persuading Elizabethan pipe-smokers, like Sir Walter Raleigh, to give it up as a danger to

Did You Know?

Incidentally, King James was one of very few people who thought smoking was bad for you. Nobody took any notice of him either so he slapped a tax on imported tobacco and profited handsomely from other people's addiction.

Education and Employment Opportunities

> **Top Tip**
>
> The Tudors even have a word for it. 'Astounded' originally meant having suffered a blow to the head that caused you to 'see stars'.

their health. Besides, Sir Walter doesn't live long enough to develop lung cancer from his habit because King James I – a Stuart not a Tudor – has him executed in 1618 after Queen Elizabeth had him imprisoned in the Tower of London at the end of her reign in 1603.

Returning now to possibilities in the field of science, there is definitely room for new inventions: anything from the 'equal to' symbol (=) to navigational aids and perhaps you can introduce ideas of your own. Magnifying glasses have been around for centuries and reading spectacles were invented in the 1280s, but glasses to aid short-sighted folk like me would be marvellous – if you know how. On the subject of improving eyesight, many older science text books give Galileo credit for inventing the telescope. He didn't. He pinched the idea from a Dutchman and demonstrated the wonderful instrument to the Doge of Venice, telling him it was a weapon of war to make it possible to spot your enemy on the horizon before the enemy can see you. Only later in the 1600s did Galileo think of using the telescope to look at the stars and planets. However, two Englishmen, father and son, probably beat Galileo to studying the stars with an instrument to help their eyes see more.[2]

Star-gazing

The universe had been explained long ago: God created the heavens and the Earth and no sensible Tudor questions that. God has fixed the stars on crystal spheres that surround the Earth like the layers of an onion. The crystal spheres are perfect, transparent and invisible, carrying the stars, set in their eternal constellations or patterns, circling the Earth, making music too beautiful for man's ears to hear as they revolve. Each planet is attached to its own crystal sphere, closer to the Earth than the star-studded sphere in this order: the Moon, Mercury, Venus, the Sun, Mars, Jupiter and Saturn. This design means the planets can move independently of each other but still travel around the Earth at the centre in perfect circles, as God originally intended. Only below the Moon, in the realm where God has given mankind influence and free will, do things change, while the universe beyond remains eternally perfect and constant, as God created it in the beginning. Beyond the sphere of fixed stars lies the realm of God and his angels.

But this view begins to be questioned in the sixteenth century. In 1543, the Catholic priest, Nicolaus Copernicus, publishes his book *De Revolutionibus* – only giving his permission to publish as he lay on his deathbed to avoid any repercussions. He thought that the Sun, not the Earth, sat at the centre of the universe. This is heresy but he insists it's merely a theory, so the Roman Catholic Church lets it pass and, for the time being, few take much notice of this incredible new idea. The thought that God might not have put mankind on his home world at the very centre of everything isn't an easy concept for the average God-fearing Tudor to even contemplate. But another shock is in store – and this one is more difficult to ignore.

Meteors – shooting stars – and comets are viewed as acts of God but, being irregular and, at this time, unpredictable events, they are believed to happen in the skies just overhead, beneath the Moon, where changes are acceptable. Comets in particular are God's way

Did You Know?

Today we know this wasn't a new star but an old one – previously too faint to see – which exploded in its death throes. The remnants of the star 'Tycho' can still be seen with modern telescopes in the X-ray band of the spectrum.

of warning man of forthcoming calamities, so it's thought. But then, in the early winter of 1572, something occurs that stuns everyone. God's perfect and unchanging universe changes! A new star, bright as Venus, appears on the crystal sphere of fixed stars, in the constellation of Cassiopeia. How can this be? Has God realised his perfect Creation needs to be improved with an extra star? Surely God can't have had a rethink of His celestial handiwork? And worse still, the new star begins to fade and disappears again about eighteen months later.

What are men to think of an infallible God who now dithers in indecision, tinkering with the universe? The world is witnessing an exploding star or *supernova*. But the Tudor astrologists haven't predicted the phenomenon so it's seen as a 'disaster', a *dis-aster* (a Latin word) meaning any event 'against the stars' or not foretold by them. Worrying as this is, some people try to rationalise the unthinkable and explain the universe in new ways.

Thomas Digges [*c*.1546–95] is one of the first Englishmen to read Copernicus' book. He thinks it makes more sense if the Earth and other planets go around the Sun but so few people have read *De Revolutionibus* that Digges publishes an English translation of the important bits from the Latin. At last, his fellow Tudors are finally introduced to the idea of the Sun-centred universe thirty years after its first appearance. Digges' book, *Prognostication Everlasting* (1576) contains the author's own thoughts concerning the universe as well. Let's ask Master Digges about his incredible new ideas:

> 'Good evening, Master Digges. May I call you Thomas to avoid confusion with your father, Leonard Digges? I believe Copernicus liked to work out his theories on paper but you think observing the night sky is more important. Tell us about that.'
>
> 'I've been studying the Milky Way for years and I'm convinced that Copernicus is right about the sun being at the centre of the universe but everyone is wrong about the stars. I don't believe they're fixed to an invisible crystal

sphere. That's just pretty poetical nonsense. I know that the stars are spread in all directions across the sky, into infinity. And I realise an infinite universe is a shocking new idea but—'

'It certainly is.'

'Don't interrupt. Not only does the Milky Way consist of innumerable stars but each one is another sun, just like our own. In fact, it's quite possible that there are other worlds like Earth. What about that?'[3]

'But, Thomas, how is it that you can see things in the heavens that nobody else has ever noticed? This infinity of stars, for example.'

'Ah, well we – my father and I – have a method of observation never tried before. My father, Leonard Digges, invented 'proportional glasses'. I know you've never seen or heard of such things but with these my father discovered things far off. We can read letters and count coins up to seven miles away! And, if we want to, we can even watch what's going on in 'private places', there and then. Not that we do that sort of thing, of course. I prefer watching the stars with my proportional glasses. Using them, I've seen that the Milky Way is made of thousands of individual stars stretching away, into infinity. You can't see that with the naked eye.'

'And you call these items proportional glasses? Can't you think of a better name for such a marvellous invention? You could call it "a telescope".'

'Mm, maybe. I think my father prefers to call them proportional glasses. Anyway, in my new book, *Prognostication Everlasting*, I'm including a double page spread showing how the Sun is orbited by the planets and the Earth is orbited by the Moon, all on their circular paths, but the rest of the diagram is scattered with random stars to the edge of the paper. This is my

Education and Employment Opportunities

revolutionary view of the universe. No one before has dared to suggest God's creation could be haphazard and disorganised nor infinite.'

'Well, thank you, Thomas, for this fascinating interview. I'm sure our readers will be intrigued by your ideas. It's fortunate that in England these days your writing isn't considered heretical, as it would be in France or Spain.'[4]

So it's a possibility that the Digges family had a telescope thirty years before such a thing was officially invented. Despite these advances, it's odd when you realise that even basic things, like the times tables, aren't taught in Tudor schools, so knowing them – without the aid of a calculator – will put you at the top of the class. Perhaps you can help your fellow students by writing them out, long-hand – you can then have them printed and sell copies!

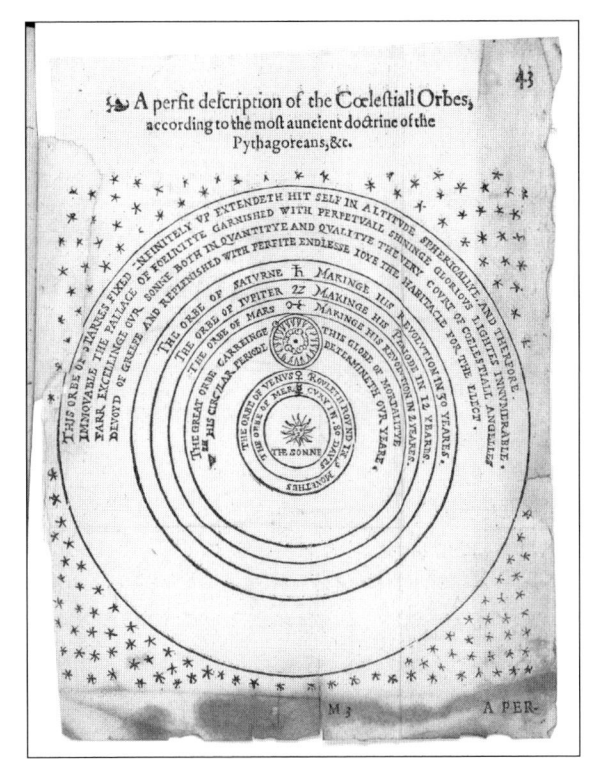

Thomas Digges's version of the universe, showing stars spreading to infinity, 1576.

Going to school

Tudor education begins at home where mothers are expected to guide their children. Don't worry if you're still young enough but don't fancy going to school – it's not compulsory in Tudor times. Anyway, you probably know enough to manage any academic study without too much trouble. Except for one thing – it'll all be taught in Latin. So if you hope to attend a Tudor university, and Oxford or Cambridge are the only choices except for Gresham College in London which opens at the very end of Queen Elizabeth's reign, learning some Latin before you go will be a great help. One other big hurdle for half of us is that more advanced schooling is for boys only, so disguise might be necessary for some. If you do decide to sit in on a few lessons, here is what to expect.

First are the Petty Schools which teach the elementary stuff. These 'little' or 'petit' schools are usually held in the teacher's own house and are sometimes known as 'dame schools' because the teacher is often a literate woman, so this may be suitable employment for female readers. The dame teaches the youngest children – boys and girls – to read and write in English, the catechism and good manners. Before the Reformation – see Chapter 4 – the catechism is the basic knowledge you need to be a good Roman Catholic: the Paternoster, the Ave Maria, the Credo, the Ten Commandments and something about the sacred sacraments of the Church, such as baptism and confirmation – in Latin. After the Reformation, in Edward VI's reign, it's all in English because everyone is now a member of the Church of England: the Lord's Prayer, the Apostles' Creed and the Ten Commandments which you'll learn by heart, but the Ave Maria is dropped and the Christian sacraments are simplified.

After petty school, at age 7, boys move on to Grammar School. Before the Reformation, most of these are run by religious establishments and many close down when the abbeys are abolished. But Edward VI, himself a very well-educated youngster, still wants his subjects to attend schools so many 'King's Schools' are founded

Education and Employment Opportunities

in his reign and still exist in the twenty-first-century, for example at Canterbury, Rochester and Grantham.

In our own time, state schools have the National Curriculum to make certain all students learn the same basic subjects but this isn't a new thing. Henry VIII had chosen and authorised just one particular Latin grammar book to be used in all schools, written by William Lily, so everyone would learn the same version of Latin nouns, verbs, etc. Lily was the first 'high master' of St Paul's School in London and died in 1522 but his book was approved by the king in 1538 and was used in schools until the nineteenth century. That's quite a memorial, isn't it? And copies still exist today. We know Shakespeare is taught *Lily's Grammar* because he mentions its text in some of his plays.[5] In 1558, a 'speller' is introduced to help children with their English spelling. This is the first effort made to improve the consistent spelling of English words from the medieval 'spell-it-however-you-think' method.

From 10 years of age to 14, boys are expected to be able to translate Latin into English and vice versa. Latin literature, drama and poetry are taught from the classical writings of Horace, Virgil and Cicero, among others. History is also likely to begin with Suetonius' book *The Lives of the Caesars*, so Tudor students know all about the Romans. They might learn other languages, such as French or even Ancient Greek, as well as arithmetic, geometry, philosophy, music and, of course, religious studies. School days begin at seven in the morning and can continue until six at night, with a dinner break around midday, including Saturdays. Books are often shared because there aren't enough for one each and much has to be learned by heart and recited in class. Beatings with a bunch of twigs – birchings – are common for those who can't memorise the lessons properly, inattention, bad manners and any other offence the master thinks deserving of punishment. And nobody complains because physical discipline is thought to be part of the learning process.

At 14, if he intends to continue his education, a Tudor lad goes to university. Or he might begin an apprenticeship to learn a trade or craft, to become a wealthy merchant like Sir Thomas Gresham, or a humble butcher like Thomas Wolsey's father. Another possibility is to attend law school at the Inns of Court in London. These inns are not just training schools for future lawyers, but give 'further education' opportunities for young gentlemen. A little knowledge of the law often comes in handy when dealing with money and property and you will polish up your manners, fashion sense and courtly behaviour as well – just in case royalty ever summons you.

If Oxford or Cambridge Universities appeal to you, you will need to have covered the Latin basics listed above and you'll now learn what to do with all that knowledge with classes teaching Logic and Rhetoric. Logic means working out and assembling arguments for and against whatever ideas or theories are being discussed, such as Copernicus' Sun-centred universe. Rhetoric teaches you how to speak well and explain your arguments clearly. These things are vital because all examinations are *viva voce* – no written exams; they are all face to face, answering questions asked by the professors there and then.

Then you can specialise in three main subjects: Theology, Medicine or Law. Medicine, though, covers a wide range of knowledge. Although based on the ancient works of Classical writers like Hippocrates, Galen and Aristotle, and some Jewish and Muslim sources too, astronomy/astrology is included as well, so that the patients' horoscopes can be drawn up and their future recovery – or otherwise – be known before treatment begins. No Tudor doctor wants to treat a patient if he's going to die and ruin their reputation as a man skilled in medical matters.

Employment opportunities without academic qualifications

In Tudor times, there are plenty of opportunities for those who haven't attended university or even a grammar school. There is also a very new skill available for young ladies to learn: starch making.

If starch hadn't been invented, the extravagant Elizabethan ruff could not exist.

A Dutch woman, Dinghen van den Plass, comes to London as a refugee in 1564 and brings with her the art of starching linen. Simple neck ruffles, as worn by Henry VIII, become finer, more intricate in construction and folding, as starch becomes a vital commodity for the wealthy. Usually made from wheat flour, during times of shortage after a poor harvest, starch production means less flour for bread. The government try to ban its production in England but, since they also slap a heavy tax on imported starch, the eventual answer is the less extravagant neckwear of the Stuart period. Meanwhile, the daughters of wealthy Tudors learn the art of starching from the Dutchwoman; Stow says they pay her £4–£5 for a course of lessons. Starching is obviously a suitable job for a woman of means and good social standing, although Philip Stubbs, in 1583, declares that 'the devil, in his malice, invented these great ruffs', regarding starch as Satan's own creation.

Having seen the complexity of steel rods that had to be heated to 'iron' in the pleats on Elizabeth I's ruffs, I suspect her laundresses may well have agreed with Stubbs that starch was invented by the devil. John Gerard, the gardener – see below – says 'the most pure white starch is made from the root of arum lily but it is most hurtful to the hands of the laundress as it blistereth and maketh the hands rugged and withall smarting'.

A tally iron: a poker-shaped iron used to shape and starch collars, ruffles and laces.

Another possible job is that of a commercial gardener. Plant nurseries are first set up in the Tudor period, growing fruit, vegetables and flowers, particularly around London. Gentlemen like to have the latest fashionable plants in their gardens, just as they want the latest in fashionable clothes. With new species coming from abroad, to have a rare specimen growing in your flower bed is something to boast about. Henry VIII, though, seems to be traditional in his choice when, in 1546, the Keeper of the King's Garden is instructed to buy 3,000 red rose trees at 3s 4d per thousand. Flowers are loved, not only for their beauty, but most especially for their fragrance. With Tudor houses being without sanitation, plants that disguise the smell with their perfume are strewn on the floor, arranged in the empty hearth in summer, worn as chaplets or garlands by ladies and carried as nosegays by churchmen, judges and gentlemen to sniff when obnoxious pongs become too much. If you have green fingers, gardening could be the job for you.

Flowers aren't everything. The Tudors like ornamental gardens to show off their status, not just as people but to demonstrate how mankind can force Nature to obey his wishes. Order and structure are imposed on plants as never before, the Tudor knot garden – an idea

Tudor knot garden at Penshurst Place, Kent, home of the Sidney family.

that had come from Italy – being a way of showing control of what would otherwise be a wild and haphazard collection of plants.

In 1575, Robert Dudley, Earl of Leicester, has a wonderfully romantic garden created at his home of Kenilworth Castle in Warwickshire for Queen Elizabeth. She is only visiting for three weeks in July but Robert still has hopes of winning the queen's hand in marriage, wooing her with fireworks and other extravagant entertainments with the garden as the backdrop. With fountains and arbours, the perfume of gillyflowers and carnations, birdsong and heraldry and no expense spared, I'm afraid the earl's efforts come to nothing.

To discover the plants growing in Tudor gardens, John Gerard's *Herball or General Historie of Plantes,* tells us everything we need to know, including illustrations of some of the newer or more interesting ones. Gerard lists some of the plants in his garden in 1596 which included thirty species of tulip, newly introduced in

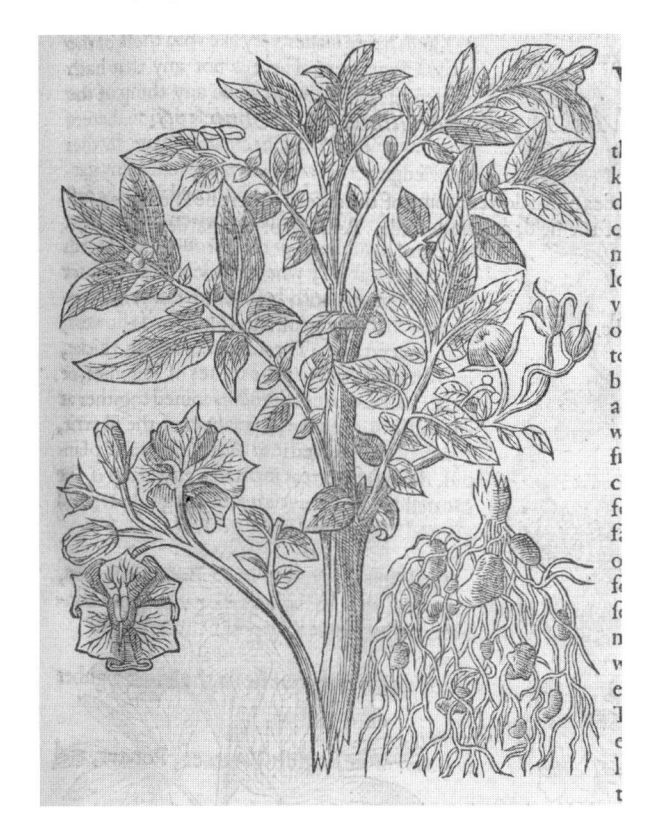

John Gerard's illustration of a Virginia potato plant, 1596.

1578, twelve daffodil species and ten iris. Spring bulbs like these become very popular in the gardens at Hampton Court Palace where Master Huggens is Keeper of the Royal Gardens. Gerard has sixteen species of roses and is the first to mention the sunflower, the Crown Imperial, hyacinths, nasturtiums and the 'very faire and pleasant' flower of the Virginia potato, newly introduced in 1585. It's odd that he thinks of potatoes as flowers, but he does note that potatoes are wholesome to eat 'being either roasted in the embers or boiled and eaten with oil, vinegar and pepper, or dressed some other way by the hand of a skilful Cook'.[6]

Perhaps you'd prefer to be a cook? Maybe you can invent chips?

Chapter 4

Religion – A Tudor Minefield

The way things were before

When the first Tudor king, Henry VII, comes to the throne in 1485, the subject of religion in England – as in most of Western Europe – is fairly straightforward: everyone, with very few exceptions, is a Roman Catholic, owing spiritual allegiance (and paying a tax) to the Pope in Rome. There are those who think things should change a bit. They argue that Christ was a poor man yet the Pope, as His representative on earth, lives a life of luxury at the parishioners' expense, getting richer still by selling 'indulgences'. Indulgences are pieces of paper forgiving you your sins, sometimes in advance before you've even committed them – a sort of 'Get-out-of-jail-free card' for Hell. Many don't approve of indulgences, arguing that only God can forgive sins.

Also, why are church services conducted, and the Bible written, in Latin which few ordinary folk can understand? Who says the prayers of common people have to be conveyed to God by a priest and not spoken directly? Surely, God can understand English: after all, He knows everything. Most people just go on, worshipping God, attending church and respecting the Pope and priests, as they have for a thousand years, but these are some of the questions floating on the wind across Christendom.

King Henry VIII is quite happy with things the way they are and even writes – with help from his archbishops – a paper in support of the Pope, saying these arguments are irrelevant. Pope Leo X is so pleased with Henry's paper that in 1521 he sends him a gift of a golden rose and awards him a fine new title: 'Defender of the

Faith' – a title still held by the British monarch in the twenty-first century, although the 'Faith' referred to is now Protestantism.

All is well until Henry realises his wife, Queen Katherine of Aragon, is getting too old to have children and hasn't yet given him the vital son and heir to continue the Tudor dynasty. Why hasn't God seen fit to give him – the perfect Christian king – a fine, legitimate son? Clearly, he must have upset God somehow. What's a king to do? In 1530, Henry asks the Pope to grant him a divorce from Katherine so he can marry his new mistress, Anne Boleyn, who will give him the son he so urgently needs. A lot of diplomatic wrangling begins, bribes go into the papal coffers but, to cut a long story short, the Pope says 'No'. Divorce isn't recognised by the Roman Catholic Church except in exceptional circumstances and the need of a male heir isn't good enough, although it might have been if Queen Katherine's nephew wasn't holding the pontiff hostage at the time. You can see the difficulty.

This is known as the king's 'Great Matter': a juicy scandal with the majority of English people taking Queen Katherine's side. She has been a loving, loyal and faithful wife to the king, serving him well in every way, except for the lack of a male heir. Is that her fault? Unfortunately for Katherine, the way conception is understood at the time, it is. After all, Bessie Blount has given Henry an illegitimate son, so the fault can't lie with the king, can it? Many people feel sorry for Katherine and see Anne Boleyn as the intruder in the royal marriage but no one realises what profound changes the king's infatuation will have on all their lives.

Henry loses patience with the Pope, desperate for that divorce. Cardinal Wolsey has had no success in persuading the Pope and falls from favour but his replacement as the king's secretary, Thomas Cromwell, has a revolutionary idea. Suppose the king is in charge of the Church in England and not answerable to the Pope in Rome? He can then do what he likes; grant himself a divorce. Not only that but he can abolish the tax paid to Rome, which will please the people, and all the wealthy monasteries will, technically, belong to him as the new Head of the Church in England, so he can sell them off. And Henry needs that cash. The process takes time but this is just what happens. In 1534, Parliament passes the Act of Supremacy, making Henry Head of the Church of England, a Protestant Church over which the Pope has no authority. Henry gets his divorce from Katherine, marries Anne Boleyn and begins closing down the monasteries to acquire their lands, properties and wealth. This is the Dissolution, or dissolving, of the abbeys and priories and is all part of the Reformation of religion in this country. Suddenly, everyone is supposed to be a Protestant, not a Catholic any longer.

In early Tudor times, the existence of Heaven and Hell is a certainty and the soul of anyone who dies without the benefits of the Last Rites and Extreme Unction is in danger of spending an eternity in torment and agony. Can you imagine the very real terror that possibility must arouse in the dying and their loved ones left behind? So wills are drawn up and charitable bequests made to ensure that doesn't happen. For the wealthy, an entire chantry chapel might be set up and priests' wages paid to have masses said, sometimes for evermore, to hasten a soul to heavenly bliss. Even poor folk might donate a tablecloth to make cleaning cloths for the chalices or money for a candle to burn before the image of their favourite saint, so the saint will intercede for them, putting in a good word with God. Donations made to the poor require them to pray for the donor's soul in return.

Did You Know?

'Protestants' are protesting against the wrongs of the Catholic Church. The Roman Catholics are generally in agreement with each other about what they believe and how religious services should be carried out. But among Protestants there is far more disunity and disagreement as to what needs to be reformed – hence numerous Protestant sects emerge: Anglicans, Calvinists, Lutherans, Quakers, Puritans, etc.

When, in the twenty-first century, we think about the changes that Henry's break with Rome caused, we know it ended England's connection with the papacy and led to the Bible being written and services conducted in English, not Latin. This sounds very positive to us but what will you find if you live in the late 1530s when all these changes are happening? People were raised believing all those things I've mentioned. A loved one has recently died. His soul is safe as it is prayed for daily by a priest, the Grey Friars and St John because he left money in his will to that effect. Now, the king is saying chantry priests are abolished, the friaries dissolved and no more candles are to be lit before saints. Suddenly the loved one's soul is in jeopardy. And what of the living when their time comes? All those precautions taken for generations are swept away because the king says so. Imagine the uncertainty, the fear and trauma felt by the people of Tudor England. A king's change of heart has destroyed their entire belief system.

The Dissolution of the Monasteries may free up vast wealth and tracts of land for the Crown to redistribute but it leaves an entire stratum of society without hope. Gradually, realising the need, the state sets up schools and hospitals but no one wants responsibility for the poor. Henry's Reformation leaves his most vulnerable subjects scared, bewildered, uncared for and with nowhere to go for assistance.

Lesnes Abbey, Bexley, Kent, one of the first to be closed down.

Don't speak out about what monarchs are doing

And what of those who disagree with what King Henry VIII is doing to the monasteries and changing England's religious scene so drastically? Some dare to speak out against his replacing the Pope as Head of the Church, denying the Act of Supremacy as being illegal. The king cannot allow anyone to openly defy him, not even men who are his friends and have served him well for years.

One who refuses to obey Henry on this matter and wishes to remain a Roman Catholic is Sir Thomas More. Let's speak to him in his prison cell at the Tower of London:

> 'Good evening to you, Sir Thomas. May I interrupt your prayers for a few minutes?'
>
> 'No, my prayers are far more important – and in proper Latin. None of your heretical English nonsense. Be off with you. Leave me to make my peace with God as the condemned man.'

Sir Thomas More.

'That's what I want to ask you about. You served as the king's Lord Chancellor and were his friend, weren't you? You both approved of the burning of six would-be Protestants for reading the New Testament in English but now Henry supports that idea. How does it feel to have him turn against you and accuse you of high treason?'

'Treason? Pah! How can it be treason to consider the Pope as Head of the Church? It has always been so. But I don't blame the king. He is misled by bad advice from that minion of Satan, Thomas Cromwell. This is all his doing … the Devil works through Cromwell and no good will come of it.'

'What of Anne Boleyn? Some blame her for the king's actions. And you refused to attend her coronation. You snubbed her as queen.'

'Aye, but she's only queen because she bewitched Henry and I can't foresee a good end for her, either. She's a Protestant heretic and will suffer for her faults, if not in this life, then in the next. All women should follow the example of my daughter Margaret: devout, educated, meek as a woman ought to be and devoted to me, of course. She visits me here as often as possible, bringing me comfort. We pray together for the salvation of all Protestant sinners, including the king, that they will see the error of their ways.'

'And tomorrow – the sixth of July 1535 – you have your appointment with the executioner. Oh, sorry, that was rather tactless of me…'

'It's a fact and I shall die the king's good servant but God's servant first. Margaret has promised my head won't be left to rot on a spike on London Bridge. I don't deserve that ignominy, but I wonder what the world will think of me.'

'Well, Sir Thomas, I probably shouldn't tell you this but I don't see what harm it can do now: in 400 years time, the Pope will canonise you as a saint and, eventually, you'll become the patron saint of statesmen and politicians. How do you like that?'

'I don't like liars and charlatans one bit. Get out, you false prophet; you heretic; you witch! You think you can tell the future? My boot is a better fortune teller and it determines that you are about to be kicked out the door. Guards! Remove this, this … abomination.'[1]

Sadly, that interview did not go quite as I hoped. Never mind, with the Dissolution well underway, there are new opportunities to better yourself by buying ex-Church property. In the twenty-first century, many grand houses still carry the name 'Abbey', a reminder that they were once a religious establishment. Anglesey Abbey, north

Anglesey Abbey, near Cambridge [GRM 2021].

of Cambridge, was once an Augustinian priory founded in the early 1100s. It is closed and dissolved in 1536. By 1595, the Fowkes family have converted it into a modern Elizabethan house, using parts of the Chapter House in the new building. Once you have a fine house, you qualify as a gentleman – or lady – and you have 'arrived' in Tudor society.

A Bible in English

One thing the Protestants do agree on is that everyone should be able to read the Bible in their own language. Despite breaking with the Roman Catholic Church, Henry VIII isn't so keen on this idea – after all he's fluent in Latin so doesn't need a translation. Also, he agrees with the Pope that laymen might misunderstand God's meaning, if they don't have a priest directing them to a correct interpretation. Protestants insist that every devout Christian 'is his own priest' and God will see to it that he understands the text in the right way. That said, it seems there are as many different nuances of meaning as there are Protestants and some interpretations are more dangerous than others, so be careful if you make your religious ideas, if you have any, known to others.

In 1522, before King Henry broke from Rome, the scholarly priest William Tyndale decided to translate the Bible into English, working directly from the original Hebrew texts for the Old Testament and the original Greek texts of the New Testament, arguing that God had given the Hebrews the Bible in their own language, so it was only right everyone else should have the same benefit. Tyndale tells the Bishop of London at the time, Cuthbert Tunstall, what he intends to do but is refused permission to produce this 'heretical' text in England, so he moves to the Continent. His work becomes the first English biblical translation to be mass-produced using printing but it's never a complete Bible. As Tyndale finishes the New Testament but is only halfway through the Old Testament in

Cologne, he is betrayed to the authorities and flees to Worms, where the first complete edition of his New Testament is published in 1526. He notes that he could have made use of Wycliffe's Lollard Bible from the 1380s, but says the English used there is too old fashioned for his 'modern' readers.

Tyndale's translations are condemned in England, his work banned and copies burned, but others are smuggled into England and widely read. Thomas More reads one and says that Tyndale has purposely mistranslated the ancient texts to promote his, at the time, heretical Protestant views. Tyndale admits his reason for creating the translation is to 'cause a boy that driveth the plough to know more scripture than the clergy of the day', many of whom are no better educated than their parishioners.

In 1531, Tyndale is living in poverty-stricken exile, although he's relatively safe in the English House, which functions like an embassy in Antwerp, where the inhabitants are supposed to have diplomatic immunity. But in the spring of 1535 a 'debauched and villainous young Englishman wanting money', by the name of Henry Phillips, gains Tyndale's trust. Phillips has gambled away all the money given him by his father and fled abroad. He promises the authorities of the Holy Roman Emperor – the ruler of Antwerp at the time – that he will betray Tyndale for cash. On the morning of 21 May 1535, having arranged for imperial officers to be waiting outside, Phillips persuades Tyndale to leave the English House. He is immediately arrested and languishes in prison for the rest of the year.

Despite the best diplomatic attempts of Henry VIII's secretary, Thomas Cromwell, to have Tyndale released and returned to the English House, he is defrocked in an elaborate public ceremony and turned over to the civil authorities to be strangled to death and burned at the stake as a Protestant heretic in October 1536. His Bible translation is unfinished. His last words are said to have been, 'Lord! Open the King of England's eyes.'

Meanwhile, Tyndale's work is continued by his friend, Miles Coverdale, who works alone to produce the first complete English

> **Did You Know?**
>
> Coverdale's translation of the *Book of Psalms* in his 1535 Bible has remained in use in the *Book of Common Prayer* down to the present day, and is retained with various minor corrections in the 1926 Irish Book of Common Prayer, the 1928 US Episcopal Book of Common Prayer, and the 1962 Canadian Book of Common Prayer, and other versions of the Anglican Prayer Book.

Bible in print. Coverdale isn't so good at the ancient Hebrew and Greek so he uses Latin, English and German sources plus Tyndale's translations. In 1534, Canterbury Convocation petitions Henry VIII that the whole Bible might be translated into English. Consequently, in 1535, Coverdale dedicates his complete Bible to the king, having it printed in Antwerp, the first edition published on 4 October 1535.

Finally, Tyndale's prayer is answered when the Great Bible, mostly his English translation of the Hebrew and Greek Scriptures, is authorised by Henry VIII in August 1537. But by 1539 Henry has announced his desire to have it 'corrected', a process which Archbishop Cranmer instructs scholars at Oxford and Cambridge Universities to undertake. If you are familiar with the Bible that is known in the twenty-first century as the King James version, you could get a job working on Cranmer's corrections. This work becomes the basic text for King James's translation of the next century, so you'll be ahead of the game, knowing the final preferred version already.

Despite allowing the Bible to be read in English, in 1538 King Henry issues a proclamation forbidding any free discussion of the meaning of the Holy Sacrament (the Communion service) and clerics are not to marry – on pain of death. But in 1547, the new king, Edward VI, has no such qualms. He is the first English monarch to be born, raised and educated as a Protestant and has no love of the Catholic religion. Edward sweeps away the remnants of the old religion to which he has no allegiance or sentimental attachment. By 1549, he has written a treatise on the Pope as the Antichrist, so there is no doubt of the young king's Protestant beliefs, and he approves Archbishop Cranmer's *Homily of Good Works* which lists the popish practices and superstitions that are to be abandoned, to better keep God's commandments.

Young Edward VI's regency council are far more enthusiastic about Protestantism than Henry was, and so is the new king. In his short reign, all the trappings of Catholicism are to be removed from churches. Sadly, this includes whitewashing over medieval wall paintings and destroying religious statues and icons – things that can never be replaced. It also means that churchmen are to be plainly dressed in sombre black and white and are expected to marry. Catholic priests are forbidden to wed, but Protestant ministers should have a wife. This is thought to make them more respectable because they won't be led into temptation by other men's wives, or prostitutes.

The list of banned items and practices includes the use of rosaries and Books of Hours, feigned relics, bells, bread, holy water, palms and candles, except for two on the altar, and the existence of Purgatory is to be denied. Fasting for Lent is no longer compulsory – a relief to many, no doubt. All these changes are made official in a set of royal Injunctions issued in the summer of 1547, many simply repeating what was proclaimed by Henry VIII back in 1538, such as the removal of relics, idolatrous images, pictures and paintings from churches and a ban on pilgrimages. But the new rules are more radical – among the images to be destroyed, stained glass windows are now included and any religious pictures or statues kept in parishioners' homes. Also, all processions with which High Mass every Sunday and major feast days always begin are no longer allowed.

The rood screens that divide the chancel from the nave, the clergy from the parishioners during the church services are now to be removed. As far as Protestants are concerned, the popish act, the so-called miracle, of transubstantiation, in which the bread and wine *become* the body and blood of Christ, had always been conducted secretly by priests, out of sight of the congregation – a ploy that revealed no miracle actually occurs. To the Protestant mind, the bread and wine are simply blessed as *symbols* of Christ's body and blood and there is no reason to conceal the simple procedure behind a rood screen. These beautiful creations, often exquisitely carved, gilded and painted, surmounted by the Rood itself – the depiction of Christ on the Cross – with the Virgin Mary and Saint John on either side of the dying Christ, are the parishes' pride and joy and their demolition is opposed by many.

If you can bear it and want to please the authorities, you could join in this destruction of the past, but have a care if you do. In London, to avoid public outcry, the fabulous rood screen in St Paul's Cathedral is removed under cover of night on 17 November 1547. Working in the dark, the huge Rood is dropped from the loft above the screen and falls on two workmen, killing them both – an event seen by many as God's judgement on such an act of sacrilege. Elsewhere, parishioners

The Rood Screen at Ripon Cathedral, Yorkshire.

attack those who come to destroy the beautiful works of art they and their ancestors have paid for and which have adorned their local church for decades, even centuries. This aspect of Protestantism is definitely not universally popular and you can understand that point of view, but you speak out at your peril. But just as Tudor people are getting used to a Protestant church, in 1553 Edward dies and is succeeded by his elder half-sister, Mary, daughter of Katherine of Aragon and a devoted Roman Catholic.

Changing times

It's all change for religion as Mary does everything possible to reinstate Catholicism, including having the Pope restored as Head of the English Church in 1554. Some people are delighted, others appalled and almost everyone is confused. Now is a dangerous time to be a known Protestant. Mary calls them heretics and has over 200 Protestants burned at the stake for refusing to return to the Old Religion, including Thomas Cranmer, Archbishop of Canterbury, author of the Protestant Prayer Book still in use in the twenty-first century.

Churches do what they can to restore the trappings of Catholicism. Some parishes have buried their ancient, sacred altars when they should have been broken up and replaced by the simple, wooden, Lord's tables preferred by Protestantism. In this case, the altar can be unearthed and put back in its rightful place. Some churches, like St Mary-at-Hill in London, pay to have the whitewash and new scriptural texts in English removed to reveal once more the pre-Reformation murals, in this case costing £4. The monks of Byland Abbey, Yorkshire, had buried the best of their sculptured saints to keep Henry VIII's men from taking them but these lay hidden in the abbey ruins until discovered in the nineteenth century and so hadn't been restored in Mary's reign.[2]

It's November 1558 and everything changes again when 'Bloody' Mary dies. Out goes papal authority in England and back comes Protestantism as Queen Elizabeth, Mary's half-sister and daughter of Anne Boleyn, comes to the throne. It's now very risky and expensive to be a Roman Catholic as fines are imposed if you don't attend a Protestant church on Sundays. Some people think God Himself is making His disapproval of Protestantism obvious when, on 4 June 1561 St Paul's Cathedral in London is struck by lightning. Its imposing steeple, said to be the tallest in Europe at between 460–520ft in height (estimates vary), is destroyed by the subsequent fire.

FACTS

A news sheet at the time reports:

Between one and two of the clock at afternoon was seen a marvellous great fiery lightning, and immediately ensued a most terrible hideous crack of thunder such as seldom hath been heard, and that by estimation of sense, directly over the City of London. ... Divers persons in time of the said tempest being on the river of Thames, and others being in the fields near adjoining to the City affirmed that they saw a long and spear-pointed flame of fire (as it were) run through the top of the shaft of Paul's steeple, from the east westward. And some of the parish of St Martin's [Ludgate] being then in the street did feel a marvellous strong air or whirlwind with a smell like brimstone coming from Paul's Church ... Between four and five of the clock a smoke was espied ... to break out under the bowl of the said shaft ... But suddenly after, as it were in a moment, the flame broke forth in a circle like a garland round about the steeple ... and increased in such wise that within a quarter of an hour or a little more, the cross and the eagle on the top fell down upon the south cross aisle ... Some counselled the remnants of the steeple to be shot down with cannons, which counsel was not liked ... Others perceiving the steeple to be past all recovery, considering the hugeness of the fire and the dropping of the lead, thought best to get ladders and scale the church, and with axes to hew down a space of the roof of the church to stay the fire, at the least to save some part of the church: which was concluded.

St Paul's steeple is never rebuilt.

Things become worse in 1570 when Pope Pius V excommunicates Elizabeth herself as a heretic. Why should she care when she isn't a Catholic? The trouble is that excommunication means no Roman Catholic is obliged to bear allegiance to her any longer and she becomes the target of assassination attempts and England is up for grabs for any European Catholic monarch who wants to invade – with the Pope's blessing. The idea is that they will be rescuing English Christian souls by bringing them back to the 'true' religion. As a result, any Catholics in England are now suspected traitors, especially priests who are seen as subversive and dangerous, plotting the queen's downfall.

With Catholic plots on everyone's mind, a London lawyer and playwright, Thomas Norton, is in charge of vetting books on behalf of the Bishop of London, checking they contain nothing seditious or pro-Catholic. He is also involved in the interrogation of Catholic priests at the Tower of London, mainly as a question-setter and note-taker, but his role is enough to earn him the unfair nickname of the 'Rackmaster', wrongly suggesting he is also a torturer. Let's ask Thomas Norton about his job:

> 'Good evening, Master Norton. Can you tell us how you come to be known as the Rackmaster? It's hardly a pleasant nickname, is it?'
>
> 'No, it isn't and I refute it utterly. I've never touched the rack at the Tower, never mind put anyone to the torture. I'd prefer to be known as a dramatist. I wrote a brilliant play, *The Tragedy of Gorboduc.* Did you know that? I wrote it while I was a law student. We students even performed it for Queen Elizabeth at Whitehall in 1561. She heartily approved it and had us repeat the performance. I wish I had time to write more plays. I'd like to be famous as a playwright, not an inquisitor. It's so unfair. I don't even disapprove of Catholics, so long as

they remain loyal to the queen. They're simply misguided heretics, in my opinion.'

'You questioned Cuthbert Mayne, didn't you?'

'I was told to do so by the Privy Council. It wasn't my idea but the man was sent to England by Pope Gregory XIII specifically to bring the papal document – called a 'bull' – telling English Catholics they no longer had to bear allegiance to her majesty. That cannot be right, can it? All subjects, no matter what their religion, must be loyal to the queen. But, mark this, I only asked questions and presented his answers at his trial. I never tortured him, neither was I judging him and passing sentence. Mayne's execution was nothing to do with me.'

'What about the priest, Edmund Campion? He was a fellow Londoner, wasn't he? What happened in his case in 1581?'

'Well the Privy Council knew he was a popular fellow and well educated by the Jesuits. They declared he should have the opportunity to understand the Jesuits' errors by debating religion with some most knowledgeable Anglican clerics. It was hoped they might convert him. I was required to find the banned Catholic books Campion wanted to research his arguments. Being in charge of vetoing books for the bishop, I knew where to find the volumes required but I told the council it would be a waste of time. Campion would never convert to Protestantism. And I was right, wasn't I? I made notes of everything said in the debate and was called as a witness at Campion's trial. He was found guilty but I refused to attend his execution at Tyburn. He was a pleasant fellow so his death was a pity.'

'You questioned the conspirator Francis Throckmorton as well.'

'I did but questioning was all. I never hurt a hair of his head. I'm no torturer and the term Rackmaster is completely undeserved. I hope posterity will call me 'Play-master' or even 'Question-master', but never that horrid title. Do what you can to persuade your readers.'

'I'll tell them 'Rackmaster' is fake news but don't hold your breath.'

'Fake news? What is that? Spy-Master Walsingham may have a use for it, if its meaning is as I suspect.[3]

So now you understand why religion is a minefield in Tudor England. I advise caution at every turn and keep quiet about theological matters. Attend church every Sunday or you may incur a fine – that's always been the case – and if you don't agree with the way the service is conducted just cross your fingers … though that may be a popish superstition, so perhaps not.

Let's leave this thorny topic now and turn to the subject of food and keeping healthy in the sixteenth century.

Chapter 5

Food and Health

Food and health are intertwined, according to the ideas of Tudor medicine and correctly so, as we understand in the twenty-first century, so this holistic approach to wellbeing won't seem too strange to you. However, what is considered a healthy diet will probably surprise you. Andrew Boorde, physician to Henry VIII, writes in detail in his new book, *Compendyous Regyment or Dyetary of Health* (1542) about the food he recommends to keep you fit and healthy. He says eating too much shortens your life and two meals a day should be enough unless you're doing hard manual labour, in which case three meals may be allowed. The physician is particularly concerned for the eating and drinking habits of Englishmen (and women no doubt, but remember it's a man's world in Tudor times):

> A lord's dish, good for an Englishman, for it makes him strong and hardy: beef, so be it the beast be young and it must not be cow flesh nor over salted. Veal is good and easily digested; boar's meat is a usual dish in winter for Englishmen.

The idea that men shouldn't eat 'cow' meat is because the flesh of a female animal is believed to be contrary to a male body. Even as babies, it is believed the breast milk produced by a woman who gives birth to a boy child is different from that produced to feed a baby girl.

Dr Boorde says bread should be of wheat alone, not mixed grains, but oatcakes are a lordly dish also. Pottage is eaten more often in England than anywhere else in Christendom and it is made by adding oatmeal, herbs and seasoning into boiling meat stock. Or an

> **Did You Know?**
>
> If a wet-nurse has to be hired because a mother can't feed her newborn, it's safe enough to have a woman who bore a boy suckle a female child, though she may grow into a bit of a tomboy, but definitely not the other way around. Otherwise the boy will grow weedy and effeminate, if he survives at all.

Englishman might enjoy a nourishing, strength-building frumenty, made by stewing meat and wheat in milk. Otherwise, milk is only good for old men, melancholy men, children and consumptives. Boorde also says that 'all meates and drinkes the which is sweet and that sugar is in, be nutrytyve', (nutritious).

A sugar loaf, Sutton House, NT, London.

As for carters and ploughmen, bacon is good for them and Dr Boorde says that slices of bacon and eggs are very wholesome for such folk, so only labourers should be enjoying 'a full English breakfast'. Being posh can have its drawbacks, I'm afraid.

Would you eat turkey for your Christmas dinner? In early Tudor times it's unlikely, but Henry VIII may have been served this rare delight from the New World. However, the ordinary people are not lacking in a choice of birds for the table at any time of year. Dr Boorde advises that:

> A bustard is nutritious meat and a bittern is not so hard to digest as a heron. Plovers and lapwings are not so nourishing as turtle-doves. Of small birds, the lark is best; thrushes are also good, but not titmouses [blue-tits] or wrens, because they eat spiders.

Before the Reformation, the Catholic Church requires that everyone – barring those with a doctor's note saying otherwise – is required to eat fish, not meat, on Wednesdays and Fridays. But Henry VIII goes a step further and rules that all Englishmen have to eat fish on Saturdays as well. This is because the fishermen of Grimsby don't know what else to do with all the herrings they catch. However, as Dr Boorde reminds readers: fish and flesh should not be eaten at the same meal, however much you may be tempted, so no 'turf-and-surf' then.

What of vegetables and fruit? The good doctor advises that Englishmen should eat turnips, parsnips, carrots, onions, leeks, garlic and radishes. Mellow red apples are very good but 'beware of green sallettes and rawe fruytes for they wyll make yowr soverayne seke'.[1] And if such foods will make his majesty ill, they must surely be unwholesome for everyone else. As for drink, Dr Boorde says some drinks are more suitable than others:

> Ale for an Englishman is a natural drink. Ale must have these properties, it must be fresh and clear, it must not

> be ropy, nor smoky, nor it must have no weft nor tail …
> Beer is made of malt, of hops and water; it is a natural
> drink for a Dutchman, and now, of late days, it is much
> used in England to the detriment of many Englishmen …
> for it doth make a man fat and doth inflate the belly, as it
> doth appear by the Dutchmen's faces and bellies. [With
> apologies to any Dutchmen.]

Note the difference between ale and beer: the latter is ale plus hops. The Dutch idea of adding hops to ale has come to England quite recently. Hops act as a preservative, so the ale keeps longer. Instead of having to brew a small batch of ale fresh every week, beer will last for months and still be drinkable. This means that brewing beer can be done on an industrial scale and men begin to take over from women as brewers. Although housewives may go on brewing ale for the family, taverns and inns start buying beer in bulk. But Dr Boorde and many others disapprove of beer. In fact, a number of brewers are prosecuted for adding 'that filthy weed hops' to their ale early in the Tudor period. Hops certainly make the sweetish-tasting ale bitter – a flavour that is thought to indicate an unhealthy food or drink.

Keeping healthy in Tudor times isn't just about diet – remember the holistic approach. Getting the right amount of sleep under the right conditions is just as important. This is Dr Boorde's advice on the subject: a healthy man shouldn't sleep during the day but if he must then 'let him lean and sleep against a cupboard, or else sitting upright in a chair'. At night, there must be a fire in the bedchamber to purify the air and consume evil vapours and the windows must be kept closed. Seven hours sleep is enough for a man, says Dr Boorde, but he must sleep on his right side with the head high; have a good, thick quilt and let his night-cap be of scarlet. To counteract fear, use merry company, rise in the morning with mirth and remember God.

So there you have the basics for keeping healthy. Oh, and Dr Boorde says you mustn't allow swearing in the house. Perhaps inventing a Tudor swear box will help the household stay well?

What is new on the Tudor menu?

As the Tudor period continues, you will see a choice of some new American imports – though probably only for the wealthy – including turkeys, avocados, aubergines, sweet and ordinary potatoes, tomatoes and sweetcorn. However, most of these foods take ages to catch on. Queen Elizabeth is said to have tried Sir Walter Raleigh's newly imported potatoes. She wasn't impressed and they didn't become popular until the eighteenth century – and then only as a food for the poor. But perhaps you can change all that by 'inventing' chips or fries. I'm sure the queen would enjoy them.

Sweetcorn, or corn-on-the-cob, maize or whatever you call it, is only used as chicken feed well into the twentieth century, but one American dish becomes popular straight away – at least with those who could afford it – turkey. The first birds are recorded in England during Henry VIII's reign. The story goes that the first turkeys are brought to England by a Yorkshireman, William Strickland, in 1526. He manages to get hold of a few birds from Native American traders on his travels and sells them for tuppence each (2d.) in Bristol, where his ship docks on the homeward voyage. But this is a one-off event. The Spaniards import far more turkeys than English merchants do and most birds sold in England in the sixteenth century come via Spain. Because this puts English silver into Spanish coffers, at the time of the Armada in 1588, when Spain and England are bitter enemies, Queen Elizabeth outlaws eating turkey in favour of goose at Christmas. 'Goose is a proper dish for an Englishman', she says.

> **Did You Know?**
>
> The trouble with both potatoes and tomatoes is that their flowers show they belong to the poisonous nightshade family of plants and this puts people off. Both do have poisonous leaves, shoots and stems.

Behave yourself at table

Whether you are eating turkey, goose, chicken or duck, you need to remember your manners at the Tudor dining table. Perhaps you may have seen, before your journey back in time, one of the most iconic movies, bringing the Tudor period alive on screen: *The Private Life of Henry VIII,* made in Britain in 1933 for London Film Productions, directed by Alexander Korda and starring Charles Laughton as King Henry. Focusing on Henry's later marriages, the film was a sensational international success, so clearly the public enjoyed this tale of Tudor affairs but beware the 'authentic' royal private life as depicted in the film. As a social historian, I'm horrified by the scenes of King Henry dining at the high table. We see a well-educated Renaissance prince ripping apart his roast chicken, gnawing the meat off the bones and flinging the remains over his shoulder, into a bystander's face. Enticing wenches flaunt themselves as they serve plates piled high with food, almost throwing them in front of the diners. Yet this image of Tudor dining is as far from the truth as another of the imaginative scenes in the film, when Anne of Cleves wins her freedom from Henry in a game of cards. So what is wrong with this raucous scene of gluttony?

It is true that Tudors don't use forks, although there are pronged tools in the kitchen for lifting meat or fish from boiling pots. Queen Elizabeth uses dainty two-pronged forks to eat sticky sweetmeats at the banquet which follows a feast. Tudor banqueting halls, follies or pavilions are for the VIPs to retire to while the servants clear the trestle tables in the great hall, ready for the entertainments. Meanwhile, the VIPs sip sweet wine, eat candied fruits, little cakes, Turkish delight and all kinds of syrupy sweetmeats – this is the 'banquet', something quite separate from the feast.

Otherwise, everyone uses fingers which have to be washed, nails cleaned and no nose-picking! Manners are everything to the well-brought-up Tudors. But let's return to chicken-gnawing Henry. Before serving, meat or fish is removed from the bone by trained carvers. In a nobleman's household, a young henchman begins his training, looking after the cups on his lordship's cupboard, making sure they are clean, untarnished and not cracked or dented. Meanwhile, he observes the roles of the pantler (in charge of bread), the butler (drink), the ewerer (handwashing water), the napier (napkins, tablecloths and towels), the cup-bearers, servers and carvers; he would progress through all departments. If a carver doesn't remove every bone and a diner finds one on his trencher, this is an appalling insult. Can you imagine taking offence at a T-bone steak or a chicken drumstick?

King Henry would be aghast, seeing a whole chicken set before him and the carver responsible would probably end up in the Tower, awaiting a degree of de-boning himself. Bones are disposed of discreetly, often fed to the dogs under the table, but they are also a saleable commodity for making glue – never thrown around. As for buxom serving wenches, they belong in disreputable taverns. At court or in a gentleman's household, the servers at dinner are all male.

Tudor dining – a family saying Grace.

Food and Health

In 1508, in London, Wynkyn de Worde publishes the first printed book on manners but it's based on a treatise on etiquette written by John Russell, a member of a noble household, sixty years earlier.[2] *The Boke of Keruinge* deals with the intricacies of carving – from tyring an egg (removing the shell) to unlacing a coney (boning a rabbit) to splatting a pike, all copied from Russell's manuscript. It covers every detail, including how to lay the posh top table with three tablecloths. The first cloth is draped down the front of the long side of the board, its edge in the centre of the board where it meets the edge of the second cloth. This second cloth drapes the laps of the diners to act as a crumb-catcher – the way we use napkins. The third cloth lies central on the board, covering the edges of the other two, and is changed at the end of each course, so the diners don't have to look at any wine spills and dribbles of sauces staining it. You can see how fussy the Tudors are.

The highest standard of personal manners shows your good breeding. Hands are washed before eating and in between courses. Napkins are for wiping greasy fingers and lips and changed at the end of each course. In the late fifteenth century, John Lydgate's manners book is printed by William Caxton (Wynkyn de Worde's master) at Westminster. Here's an extract:

> With soup, do not use bread to sop it up,
> Or suck it loudly – that is to transgress,
> Or put your dirty mouth to a clean cup,
> Or pass drinks while your hands are in a mess,
> Or stain your napkin out of carelessness.
> Also, beware at meals of causing strife,
> And do not make a tooth-pick of your knife.

Table Manners for Children, John Lydgate.

There are fourteen stanzas on this topic. Books of courtesy, as they are called, are required reading for all courtiers and social-climbers. No blowing on your soup, no belching or farting at table or laughing

> **⚲ Top Tip**
>
> Tooth-picks are fashionable and it's good manners to use one. The wealthy have silver ones and you can keep yours handy by sticking it in your hat.

with your mouth full, don't blow your nose on your napkins and never rest your elbows on the table. This last was enforced at dinnertime when I was a child and my parents could never give me a sensible answer when I asked why; 'you just don't', I was told. Now that I know the rule goes back to a time when the table was a board resting on trestles and not fixed to the legs, the reason is clear: if you lean on a trestle board, it will tip, sending food, drink and cutlery straight into your lap.

Tudor feasts are decorous affairs with dainty dishes, elegant presentation and sober waiters – at least until the serving of the 'subtlety', the last dish of each course. Wondrous contraptions of sugar-work and marzipan – like wedding cakes without the cake – these 'subtleties' are the pinnacle of the confectioner's art. Castles, dragons spitting flame, warships firing cannon, mythical figures and trick-boxes, the more elaborate the better, are paraded and admired by the diners before the folk on the lower tables are let loose, to smash the masterpieces, grab the best bits and eat them. It's a free-for-all, courtesy forgotten, at least until the trumpet announces the serving of the next course, when everyone returns to their places at table to begin fine dining once more. So don't believe history as you see it at the movies; they don't let the truth ruin a good show.

Caring for the family

So now you know what foods to expect to be served and how to eat it politely, if you're dining with the wealthy. Apart from bacon and eggs [see above], what do poorer people eat? The trouble is that because the poor are mostly illiterate, nobody bothers to write out recipes for them and, besides, girls learn all they need to know about cooking plain everyday dishes from their mothers, aunts, grandmothers and elder sisters. Family recipes are passed on by word of mouth only – which is a pity from the historian's point of view. But later in the sixteenth century, more ladies of the gentry and upper classes can read and begin writing and compiling cook books to share with their friends or pass on to the next generation. A few of these marvellous books survive into the twenty-first century, including the 'receipt' (recipe) book of Lady Elinor Fettiplace, an Elizabethan housewife from Oxfordshire. Elinor must have a beautiful garden, overflowing with roses in June and July, because she uses roses in her cooking, beauty care and remedies for the family, all made by hand, of course. Let's ask Elinor about some of her receipts made with roses:

> 'Lady Elinor, I've been reading your book of family receipts and see that you use roses for so many things. Can you tell us about some of your favourite recipes?'
>
> 'Rose petal conserve is easily the family's favourite, made with red rose petals, it has a good colour and can be used in so many ways. First, and you must remember to cut off the bitter white piece at the bottom of every single one (a chore, I know, so get your cook maid to do it). Then boil your petals in water for half an hour. For each pound of stewed petals add three pounds of sugar and boil it all together until it thickens. Then put it in glass bottles and store in the dark, so it keeps its colour. This conserve is good for treating all manner of coughs, colds and afflictions of the chest. It can also flavour water ices and sorbets in the summer to cool you on a hot day.'
>
> 'What about these new potatoes from America, my lady? Do you ever cook with them?
>
> 'Oh, yes. We rather like the sweet potatoes and I have an excellent receipt that uses them. I boil them in water

until they are quite soft, then peel and slice them. I add rosewater – for which I can give you the receipt, if you wish – and sugar and the peel and juice of an orange and boil it all together with a generous piece of butter. You may serve it straight or put it in a dish with more butter atop and bake it for half an hour to accompany your roasted meats. It is very good. I served the dish, baked, when my cousin, Sir Henry Danvers, came to dine last month. It was remarked upon by Lady Danvers who would have my receipt for it.'

'So the receipt uses roses and sugar again?'

'Of course. Both are healthful ingredients and using sugar demonstrates our family's wealth and standing. "Sugar with everything" is my motto in the kitchen. I use sugar in dishes ranging from shoulder of mutton to eel pie.'

'Sugar with eels, my lady?'

'Certainly. You skin and bone the eels and lay them in a dish with chopped hard-boiled egg yolks, currants, chopped dates, sugar, cinnamon and ginger. Add a dash of vinegar, dot with butter and bake for an hour until the fish is well cooked. My husband, Sir Richard, approves this dish particularly and it is my grandmother's receipt from before King Henry's day.'

'Many thanks, Lady Elinor. I shall definitely try the sweet potato recipe … I mean receipt. But all that sugar…'

'It's the fashionable thing, you know, to have blackened teeth to show you can afford plenty of sugar. Look at her majesty, Queen Elizabeth's teeth – black as soot and signifying her noble status.'[3]

If you have money enough and to spare, one of Lady Elinor's receipts goes all out to impress her guests. She calls it Spanish Marmalade – it's not marmalade as we know it, but little sweets

Food and Health

The kitchen at Gainsborough Old Hall, Lincs.

to be served at the end of a posh meal. It requires rosewater and sugar boiled together, then remove from the heat and stir in ground almonds and ground dates added together with ground cinnamon, half a spoonful of powdered seed pearls and three sheets of gold leaf. Stir it well, allow to go cold and cut into squares. Even the queen would be impressed with pearls and gold! Don't worry, gold is edible in that it passes straight through the body, unchanged. Dong-collectors go through the cess-pit afterwards and any gold leaf flakes they recover can be rinsed and sold back to the goldsmiths for reuse – the money they make is one of the perks of the job.

Did You Know?

On the subject of toilets, the weed 'great mullein' is grown in Tudor gardens specifically for its large, strong, soft leaves which make excellent toilet paper.

Great mullein plant – the leaves are used as toilet paper.

New diseases

The Tudor period experiences some nasty new diseases: the sweating sickness and syphilis, as well as a more virulent strain of an old one: smallpox. The sweating sickness afflicts England more frequently than any other European country and becomes known as the 'English sweat'. However, it seems to have arrived here along with Henry Tudor's mercenary troops when he invaded in August 1485 and spread like a bush fire. This deadly disease has flu-like symptoms with chills followed by respiratory problems, then a raging fever with violent sweats. The victim can be dead within a few hours. Even in the twenty-first century, the cause has not been identified for certain, mainly because, fortunately, the disease disappears as suddenly as it came in 1578.

In September 1485, the sweating sickness devastates London for the first time. A series of wills are drawn up by a group of citizens, including three fishmongers all of Bridge Street, and granted probate, i.e. the citizens have recently died, on the same day, 14 October. Most of the wills are written between the 23 and 26 September, some so brief, they are obviously drawn up in a hurry. Perhaps these men are friends and get together frequently, passing the disease among themselves.[4] Two lord mayors, three sheriffs and six aldermen also fall victim. Children and the elderly seem less vulnerable than fit, healthy adults, strangely.

The wealthy don't escape the sweat either. In another epidemic of the sweat in 1528, one of Anne Boleyn's ladies is among the first to fall ill. Henry VIII, ever terrified of disease since his brother Arthur, Prince of Wales, died in 1502, possibly of the sweat which his young wife, Katherine of Aragon, also caught but survived – to marry Henry seven years later – sends Anne home to Hever Castle in Kent. Anne and her brother George contract the disease but survive. The sons of the king's old friend, Charles Brandon, Duke of Suffolk, are far more unfortunate in the epidemic of 1551. Henry Brandon, the 2nd Duke of Suffolk, dies of the sweat on 14 July, followed on the same day by his younger brother Charles. Charles is designated 3rd Duke of Suffolk so he must have died after Henry but within hours, probably never knowing he was a duke.

Another disease which is new in the Tudor era but which has never left England, or anywhere else, in peace since is syphilis. Also known as the great pox and, depending on your point of view, the French pox, the Spanish disease, etc. – just so long as someone else is blamed. Syphilis is believed to have arrived in Europe with the return of Christopher Columbus and his crew from the Caribbean in 1492, although in the twenty-first century there is some disputed evidence that the disease was already here long before that. No matter. The fact is that if the great pox isn't an entirely new problem, it's definitely a far more significant one from the late fifteenth century onwards. It's a sexually transmitted disease, its progress in the human body is insidious and Tudor medicine – and for centuries to come – has no cure. The treatments are often as harmful to the patient as the ailment. Symptoms in the early stage may be so slight, the patient isn't even aware of them, yet they are highly contagious. In the second stage, up to two years later, the symptoms of a mild rash, sore throat and flu-like weariness can be mistaken for other minor problems, so again it can go undiagnosed but is still contagious, even during months at a time that are symptom free. It can take up to twenty years to reach the final stage which may cause blindness, madness and death. But be aware, the usual treatment is mercury which is a poison and may kill sooner rather than later. I caution you to choose your partners with care!

While you're carefully avoiding the great pox, there is also the small pox to contend with. Smallpox has been around for centuries and in the medieval period was accounted as one of childhood's 'spotted fevers' like chickenpox. Like measles, it could be fatal but most children survived unscathed, except for a few scars. However, during the later sixteenth century, we begin to hear of smallpox increasingly as a disease of adults, disfiguring and too often fatal.

And it gets worse in the seventeenth century, the royal houses of Europe being badly affected. But that's in the future.

Occasionally, sumptuary laws, known as Acts of Apparel – usually about what you're allowed to wear (see Chapter 6) – are passed because of health issues. For example, in 1543, there is a serious outbreak of some kind of disease among cattle in and around London, so the Common Council introduces legislation to limit the consumption of meat at mayoral feasts and not just of beef. To ensure the beef isn't simply replaced by an extravaganza of other costly foodstuffs, the number of courses at any feast is to be limited, depending on the status of those at the table: the lord mayor should not have more than seven dishes at dinner or supper; aldermen and sheriffs are limited to six, the sword-bearer to four and the mayor's and sheriffs' officers to three, with a fine of 40s for every extra dish. Beside this, they are prohibited from buying swan, crane or bustard, to be fined 20s for any such bird served.

In 1562, Queen Elizabeth seems to have caught a cold at Hampton Court. She becomes very feverish and when the spots appear it's obvious she has smallpox. Seriously ill – and it's feared she may die – her faithful friend, Lady Mary Sidney nurses the queen throughout and back to health. Sadly, Lady Mary's loyalty and devotion are repaid horribly. When she suffers the smallpox, unlike the queen who remained visibly unscarred – Mary is hideously disfigured. Elizabeth cannot bear to look at her faithful friend's ugly face and sends her from court. Poor Mary spends the rest of her days as a virtual recluse, wearing a mask on the rare occasions when she does socialise. The Tudor monarchs can be heartless, as we know, but this seems too cruel.

Remedies

Whatever your ailment, Sir Walter Raleigh has the recipe for a 'purely medicinal' alcoholic cordial made with tobacco which will surely make you feel better. It's good for easing pain, especially toothache,

> **Did You Know?**
>
> Tobacco was grown in England in the Elizabethan and early Stuart period. Sudeley Castle in Gloucestershire – home of Henry VIII's sixth wife, Katherine Parr after the king died – was famous for growing tobacco. However, Sir Walter's receipt says specifically that the tobacco should 'not be English' in this case.[5]

killing intestinal worms and treating chest complaints. Tobacco is worth its weight in silver, so it's a very costly remedy.

> Take 2 gallons of Muscadell [a sweet white wine], a pound of shredded tobacco leaves and a pound of ground aniseed. Leave the tobacco and aniseed to steep overnight in the wine. Heat over a gentle heat, distil off the alcohol, add some chopped 'reasins of the sun' [raisins] and drink it.

For a headache, you might give this treatment a go:

> First catch a mouse. Skin it. Burn or dry the skin then beat it to a powder and mingle with vinegar. Anoint your head when it when in pain and it will ease and help you.

Not sure it will work though…

Chapter 6

The Problems of Fashion

Being fashionable at any time during the sixteenth century can be hard work and expensive for both men and women. Discussing it in detail will fill an encyclopaedia so here I'm going to give you the basics, enough to ensure your arrival in the Tudor era won't get off to a bad start with an obvious fashion *faux pas* like wearing the wrong sort of farthingale or putting your forepart on under your kirtle. And men must be careful not to confuse their canions with their galligaskins. So here goes:

Women's dress

There are four basic layers to women's clothing. You begin with the chemise or shift, a loose garment, around knee-length and without any shaping. It's made of linen and the idea is that it soaks up perspiration and is changed and washed frequently, keeping your more elaborate and expensive over-garments from getting smelly.

Your second layer consists of a petticoat with a bodice of tight-fitting linen, usually sleeveless and stiffened with layers of buckram to give support to the breasts and create the required profile. It's fastened by being laced together through eyelets: front lacing is easiest but, if you have servants to assist you, side or back-lacing gives a smoother appearance. In 1554, the wardrobe accounts of Queen Mary Tudor lists a new petticoat for her majesty of scarlet with a bodice of crimson taffeta.

The third layer is your kirtle and, depending on fashion, parts of this garment may be on show, so a more expensive cloth is used. For

> **Did You Know?**
>
> Red is believed to be a warm, healthful colour for clothes worn close to the skin, although 'scarlet' is actually a high quality woollen cloth which isn't necessarily red. Only gradually does 'scarlet' come to refer to the colour, rather than a specific textile.

Anne Boleyn's coronation in June 1533, her kirtle is made of five yards of white satin lined with two and a half yards of red cloth, type unspecified.

Before we come to the fourth layer, the gown, you will also require knee-length stockings: woolly ones, if you're poor; silk,

George Gower's 'Armada Portrait' showing Elizabeth wearing a decorated stomacher, pearls, a red wig, padded sleeves and a ruff, c.1588.

if you can afford them. These are held up with garters, perhaps of ribbon – there's no elastic – or grand ones with 'buckles and pendants of gold' like those worn by uncrowned Queen Jane Grey when imprisoned in the Tower of London. Even as prisoners, royals have to keep up appearances and she has a perfumed purse made of sable skin sent to her as well. You may also be wondering about that eternal question: does Anne Boleyn wear knickers? Obviously, Henry VIII could answer this question for us but do you dare ask?[1]

Now we come to the gown. This is what everyone will see and it needs to impress, if you want to be noticed at court. For her coronation, Anne Boleyn wears a gown 'of right crimson satin lined with cloth of gold tissue'. 'Right crimson', or true crimson, is the brightest red and must look gorgeous set off with a gold lining which is intended to show here and there. In its simplest form the Tudor gown is an inverted cone-shaped bodice attached to a cone-shaped skirt with or without a train and with fitted upper sleeves which flair out into deep, turn-back cuffs to show the lining of fur or contrasting fabric.

While the poor hope for a woollen gown better than humble homespun, the rich may wear cloth of gold or silver, damask, silk-velvet, tinselled satin, finest wool embroidered with gold, silver and silk thread and then trimmed or lined with imported furs, such as black sable, white arctic fox or spotted lynx. Rabbit and cat fur are good enough for the common folk. Courtiers bankrupt themselves and their families, squandering their inheritances trying to outshine the likes of Robert Dudley, who spends £563 in one wardrobe spree, buying seven doublets and two cloaks.

The making of a Tudor gown involves many hands, from dyers and weavers, haberdashers and cloth merchants, to tailors and seamstresses. Then the gown requires embellishment by embroiderers, goldsmiths and jewellers to add the finishing touches with brooches, pendants, earrings, ropes of pearls – Queen Elizabeth loved pearls as a symbol of her virginity – and hair ornaments.

> **Do you know** your Spanish farthingale from your French farthingale? The Spanish farthingale is a conical hooped underskirt. The French farthingale is more barrel-shaped, fanning straight out at waist level, like the spokes of a cartwheel, and is popular at Elizabeth I's court, if far less practical for everyday wear.

So that covers the basic layers of women's dress, but other items of apparel may be in fashion at various dates. The bum-roll or 'rowle' goes in between the petticoat and the kirtle. Literally, it's a roll of cloth tied around the waist, to make the kirtle and gown flare out behind.

Then there are the partlet, stomacher and forepart – each required depending on the demands of the fashionable design of the gown. In the reigns of both Henrys, ladies' necklines are square and wide so a partlet is worn under the gown to protect your bare skin from the elements. By Elizabeth's time, the partlet may be embroidered and have separate sleeves. 'A pair of sleeves' is the perfect gift for a lover to give his sweetheart. Sleeves can be laced in place or simply pinned at the shoulder and may be slashed to show a contrasting lining or the sleeves of your kirtle. Since sleeves are detachable, the poor woman may remove hers when doing the washing or messy household tasks. The wealthy can mix-and-match sleeves and gowns to create a fresh look.

The stomacher, or placard, is a large triangle pinned to the centre of the bodice to conceal the lacing, and the forepart is an inverted triangle similarly fixed to the centre of the gown skirt. Depending on your status, both can be of plain simple fabric or highly decorated with jewels and embroidery and definitely meant to be seen when the gown is worn open at the front. I wonder how they originated? I'm tempted to think that someone had a length of gorgeous cloth that wasn't quite enough to go around them, so the too little allowances in the bodice and skirt were in-filled with contrasting cloth and a new fashion created. Perhaps you can ask someone during your visit back in time.

Accessories

No lady's outfit is complete without accessories and the most obvious is headwear of some kind. For common women, a simple coif or linen cap is worn all the time, but the well-to-do have more scope for style. Queen Elizabeth, wife of Henry VII, and Queen Katherine of Aragon favour the English gabled hood, but the rounded French hood is also worn early in the Tudor period. In the photograph below, Anne Boleyn favours the more becoming French hood but Jane Seymour reverts to the gable hood, perhaps to distinguish her profile from Anne's. Anne of Cleves prefers the German fashion, Katherine Howard and Katherine Parr the French – to judge by their portraits.

Queen Mary wears a different style of hood with a square gable, rather than pointed. In her early portraits, Princess Elizabeth wears

Henry VIII's queens showing English gable hoods and French hoods
From the right – George Boleyn, Katherine of Aragon (English hood), Anne Boleyn (French hood), Jane Seymour (English hood), Anne of Cleaves (German style headdress), Katherine Howard (French hood) and Katherine Parr (a cap and hat). Seated – Princess Elizabeth.

a French hood but by the time she becomes queen, hoods are no more as the fashionable ladies replaced them with elaborate hair – or wigs – and jaunty little hats. So at Queen Elizabeth's court you can, quite literally, let your hair down.

Another vital accessory for the wealthy is a pair of gloves. Not labourers' hard-wearing stout leather gloves, but the daintier the better. These aren't to keep your hands warm, in fact you don't need to wear them but carry them prominently so everyone can see how beautiful they are. Finest kid-skin, silk or satin, tight-fitting, bejewelled and embroidered, gloves are an ideal, flattering gift for anyone, even the queen, and especially if they're perfumed!

Scented fans and purses are very fashionable. Queen Elizabeth loves to carry a fan as it's perfect for keeping yourself cool or wafting

Elizabeth Knollys, Lady Layton, wearing a fashionable hat, 1577, attributed to George Gower.

away unpleasant smells. On one memorable occasion, her fan was extremely useful when Edward de Vere, Earl of Oxford, made a low obeisance to the queen and happened to let go an enormous fart. He was so ashamed that he left the country for seven years. Upon his return, Queen Elizabeth welcomed him with the equally memorable words: 'My lord, we had quite forgot the fart!'

The ideal Tudor beauty has milk-white skin to show she never toils outside in the sun, set off by rosy cheeks and red lips. Hair should be pale yellow, although Elizabeth, as a red-head, makes that a fashionable alternative. Those naturally blessed with pale skin can make it whiter still by being bled by a surgeon or bleaching the skin with lemon juice. But for those with a darker complexion or, heaven forbid, freckles – is the red-haired queen so afflicted? – then make-up is a possibility. A foundation layer of white lead and vinegar, possibly mixed with egg white, known as ceruse, is applied. Marvellous at hiding any scar or blemish and filling in the wrinkles so the queen can maintain her illusion of youth and virginity, ceruse is, unfortunately, poisonous. Symptoms can include high blood pressure, joint and muscle pain, difficulties with memory or concentration, headaches, abdominal pain, mood swings and fertility problems.

Once you have acquired the stark white look, you need to add colour, if only to avoid looking like a corpse. Fashionable ladies put rouge on their cheeks as blusher. This is simply more ceruse coloured with red ochre and blended into the cheeks. Lipstick is made from plaster of Paris mixed to a paste with vermilion – a mercury poison – or harmless but less vivid madder root, rolled into shape like a wax crayon and left to dry in the sun. Kohl is put on to darken the lashes – just as Cleopatra used it centuries ago.

Now for the hair-do. If you're not a natural red-head like the queen, nor a fashionable blonde, a mixture of saffron, cumin seed and celandine ground together in oil will soon achieve the desired effect or you could resort to wearing other people's hair as the queen does. Elizabeth has at least eighty human-hair wigs and hair pieces in her wardrobe. These are vital as her own hair becomes thin as she

Queen Elizabeth I wearing a ruff with stomacher and forepart, holding a fan of ostrich plumes.

ages, but they're also convenient because she can leave her stylist to work on her elaborate coiffure for tonight's feast and banquet while she gets on with more interesting things, like playing off her would-be suitors, one against the other.

The ruff – the epitome of Elizabethan fashion

The most obvious accessory of the later Elizabethan period is the ruff, worn by both men and women of all ages and classes. What begins as a modest frill gathered onto the standing collar or band of a shirt or shift gradually grows into a huge ruff, beloved by Queen Elizabeth, if her portraits are any guide. At first, the design and size of ruffs is limited but an enterprising Dutchwoman, Dinghen van den Plass, comes to London as a refugee in 1564 and brings with her the art of starching linen (see Chapter 3). Only with the advent of starch

Sir Walter Raleigh wearing a delicate ruff in a miniature by Nicholas Hilliard.

does the very elaborate ruff become possible. Simple neck ruffles develop into finer, more intricate constructions as starch becomes a vital commodity for the wealthy.

Having seen the complexity of steel rods that had to be heated to 'iron' in the pleats on Elizabeth I's ruffs, I suspect her laundresses might well wish they would swiftly go out of favour. Although the queen is always shown in her portraits wearing a ruff of virgin white, coloured ruffs are fashionable too, tinted pink or yellow by using

Top Tip

Don't wear your ruff in the rain. If the starch gets wet, you'll have a soggy mess of linen and wall-paper paste around your neck. Your servant should carry it in a band-box (band is another word for ruff, or even for clerical dog-collars and other neckwear) and pin it in place when you reach your destination, so you look splendid.

coloured starch. However, do not be tempted to wear a blue one as this is the badge of a prostitute.

And so we come to what the court gallants are wearing in hope of impressing her majesty.

Men's dress

The men of Tudor England, like the women, wear layers. Underwear consists of a linen undershirt and braies (like boxer shorts tied with a drawstring). Poorer men wear long cloth or woollen hose, cut on the bias to fit the leg closely and early on these would be two separate legs but later become a pair – more like tights – but with an opening at the front covered by the cod-flap. The hose have eyelets corresponding to those in the petticoat or doublet through which laces tie them in place to keep them up. The cod-flap is also fastened by laces. Later, in the middle of the century, younger men prefer shorter knee-length versions and then knitted hose (stockings) like over-the-knee socks.

On top of the shirt, goes the lined linen petticoat, laced down the front and to the hose. The petticoat has a deep 'V' neckline and is sleeveless. Over the petticoat you wear a doublet which is long sleeved and fitted and may have a collar and a peplum [a 'skirt']. If you're doing hard work, you can remove your doublet and roll up your shirt sleeves but don't take off your petticoat! Your next layer, over your doublet, is a woollen jerkin or a coat, this latter known as a cassock.

The rich also wear linen undergarments and petticoats. Next to your skin, you have a white linen shirt which may be embroidered, as can the petticoat, though nobody will see it except round the collar band. Later, the collar band is simply what your ruff is pinned onto, unless it has become a separate item by the time of your visit. If you're wealthy, your hose can be of silk and satin, and padding, pleating and puffing are all the rage.

The Problems of Fashion

> **📌 Top Tip**
>
> Make sure your codpiece isn't bigger than the king's and don't point or snigger at his, however absurd it looks, not if you want to keep your head.

Henry VII favours long robes of fine cloth to show his wealth but his son, young Henry VIII, famed for his athletic, shapely legs, wears fitted hose and short robes so he can show off his best features. Now that the doublet and robe are so short, the cod-flap is visible and Henry turns this into an asset by attaching a great codpiece to show off his virility. Since the courtiers take their fashion cues from the king, codpieces become a vital accessory.

Henry is a muscular, sporty, young man but even so, his natural physique is accentuated by padding the shoulders of his doublet to extreme proportions.

In this image you can see the slashes in the sleeves of the king's doublet so that little puffs of his fine shirt can be pulled through. The doublet has a skirt or peplum, of varying length according to fashion, underneath which are hidden the laces or 'points' to attach the hose.

By Elizabethan times, leg-wear changes, going in and out of fashion. Here is a selection to choose from once you've checked

Henry VIII wearing a padded doublet and codpiece, showing his fine legs.

out what your fellows are wearing today: round or French hose are short, full breeches ending anywhere between the upper thigh to just above the knee and excessively padded at the hips to accentuate your buttocks. Canions are tight fitting tubes attached to the short version of the round hose to extend them to the knee. Below the knee you wear stockings or 'netherstocks' held up with garters.

During a royal visit to Sandwich in Kent in 1573, the leading citizens were kitted out at the town's expense to welcome Queen Elizabeth; 200 outfits consisting of a white doublet, black 'gally gascoynes' and white garters were tailored to impress her majesty. These galligaskins are a more comfortable style of looser breeches that you may prefer. They are probably another fashion from France – from Gascony, as the name suggests.[3]

Whatever style you choose, your hose may be 'paned' – that is cut into narrow panels, joined at the waist and hem, with a coloured lining showing between the panes. With so much padding and paning, you can understand why, by the later Tudor period, the codpiece is in decline, giving way to a modest buttoned or lace-up opening which doesn't spoil the symmetry of your panes. Both your doublet and hose may also be decorated by 'pinking': slits cut in the fabric, in a pattern, with the coloured lining pulled through, as in Henry VIII's time. One contemporary commentator of Elizabethan men's fashion thought things had become quite ridiculous: 'Except it were a dog in a doublet you shall not see any so disguised as are my countrymen of England', he wrote and it's true that late sixteenth-century clothes disguise the wearer's true physique more than the fashions of any other period.

As you'll see in the portrait of Sir Walter Raleigh (see page 95), men also need to wear a bit of bling. Sir Walter has a large, star-shaped jewel in his modest little hat. Finger rings are a must and, for the truly fashionable man-about-town, a single earring of gold with, perhaps, a diamond to catch the light or, preferably, with a pendant pearl, if you want Queen Elizabeth to notice you.

Facial hair is also in vogue ever since Henry VIII grew a beard, but at the Elizabethan court the natural look isn't enough. Once again, Sir Walter is a fine example to copy with his beard neatly trimmed to a point and his moustache curled. Set off your ensemble with a short cape, fur-lined and edged with braid. This isn't a practical cloak to keep you warm and dry but rather an accessory to be draped nonchalantly over one shoulder for that devil-may-care look that's the height of fashion.

Footwear

No one of any significance goes without shoes. As I mentioned previously, pointy-toed, medieval styles go out of fashion almost as the first Tudor king sits on the throne. Rounded toes are the thing. But Henry VIII goes further, creating a fashion for square toes. With more leather used to make the uppers, it's also possible to have slashes to show off a contrasting inner lining, as with sleeves. However, these early Tudor styles are thin-soled and flat like their medieval predecessors but around 1500, somebody invents the 'welt' – a narrow strip of leather than goes around the shoe, in between the upper and the sole, making the shoe far more sturdy and able to withstand fancier shaping and decoration.

King Henry is tall and impressive anyway, but others who want to emulate him could do with a few extra inches in height and by the time of Elizabeth, low-heeled shoes have been invented. At first, the heel is just a wedge of cork or wood fixed between the leather sole and the upper but soon these become proper heels and part of the sole. With so much innovation in the world of shoemaking, in 1579 the queen grants their coat-of-arms to the Guild of Cordwainers in London.

Women's dainty dress shoes, called 'pinsons', now with heels and a more dainty tapered toe, can be of silk, velvet or brocade often with bejewelled rosettes. Mid-century, most are slip-ons, but laces and latchets become increasingly fashionable.

The Puritan Phillip Stubbes disapproves of pointlessly fancy shoe fashions, writing in 1583:

> They have corked shooes, pincnets, and fine pantofles, which bear them up a finger or two inches or more from the ground; wherof some be of white leather, some of black, and some of red, some of black velvet, some of white, some of red, some of green, raced, carved, cut and stitched all over with silk, and laid on with golde, silver, and such like: yet, to what good uses serve these pantofles, except it be to wear in a private house, or in a man's chamber to keepe him warme? … but to go abroad in them, as they are now used al together, is rather a let or hinderance to a man then otherwise; for shall he not be faine to knock and spurn at every stone, wall or post to keep them on his feet?

For outdoor wear you can either put overshoes on to protect your indoor footwear, or you can have leather boots for walking and riding. Loose or tight-fitting, 'gamaches' are thigh-length high boots, 'buskins' come to the calf.

Acts of Apparel

In Henry VIII's reign, realising some of the up-and-coming wealthier gentry and merchants are wearing more sumptuous clothes than noblemen and courtiers, new laws are passed, termed Acts of Apparel, in 1509–10, 1514, 1515 and 1533. Europe has similar ideas but whereas their regulations tend to be drawn up by, and apply only to, individual towns, England's laws come from Parliament and apply throughout the country – in theory, anyway.

According to the 1509–10 Act against Wearing of Costly Apparel, only the king, the queen, the king's mother (the act must have been first drawn up before Margaret Beaufort died in June 1509), along

The Problems of Fashion

with the king's brothers and sisters can wear cloth of purple silk or gold, while dukes and marquises can only use cloth of gold as linings of their coats and doublets. An earl and those of higher rank may wear sable fur, but those below may not. Certain imported furs can be worn by royal grooms and pages, university graduates, yeomen and landowners whose estates bring in an income of at least £11 per annum. Barons and knights of the Order of the Garter (the highest ranking knights) are permitted to wear woollen textiles manufactured abroad but, for those of lesser status, it's a crime to wear imported cloth. The same applies to wearing cloth dyed with the most expensive crimson and blue dyes.

Anyone who isn't a lord's son, a government servant or a gentleman with an income from land of at least £100 per annum is forbidden to wear velvet, satin or damask; although, if their land is

'Unknown Man in a Red Doublet' – too much crimson dye?

worth £20 or more, satin, damask or camlet may be used to line or trim their clothing, but not for the main, visible body of the garment.

The problem is, as it has been for centuries, more and more successful merchants are becoming richer than the aristocracy. Inter-marriage makes matters even more complex. The nobility want to share in mercantile wealth and merchants yearn for titles and high status. The solution is for a lord's penniless second and untitled son to wed the daughter of a rich merchant, but where do their offspring stand on the social ladder? The children aren't the sons and daughters of a lord and yet they can now afford to live in greater opulence than their paternal relatives who still have titles. No wonder the laws are flouted.

An additional oddity concerns the way wealth is judged. Annual income from land is always regarded as having greater status than the same monetary income gained from trade. The sumptuary laws passed in the reign of King Edward III in 1363 equated a landowner worth £200 a year to a merchant worth £1,000. These relative values are still maintained throughout the Tudor period. And there is another problem that becomes more acute in Henry VIII's reign: that of people – and courtiers were some of the worst offenders – vying with their peers to be the most fashionable and expensively dressed, and running up huge debts in the process. This situation leads to An Acte for Reformacyon of Excesse in Apparayle being passed in 1533:

> for the necessaire repressing avoiding and expelling of the inordinate excesse dailye more and more used in the sumptuous and costly araye and apparel accustomablye worne in this Realme, whereof hath ensued and dailie do chaunce suche sundrie high and notable inconveniences as to be the greate manifest an notorious detriment of the common Weale, the subvercion of good and politike order in knowledge and distinction of people according to their estates p[re]emyences dignities and degrees, and to the utter impoverysshement and undoyng of many

inexpert and light persones inclined to pride moder of all vices.

Despite the declaration that these laws are intended to avoid the 'notorious detriment of the common weal' (i.e. everyone), the legislation is aimed, as usual, at morally 'light persons inclined to pride (mother of all vices)'. The laws also reiterate earlier attempts to mark out prostitutes from respectable women but in 1533 the earlier, medieval customs of what was considered respectable attire are enshrined in law for the first time, in particular that a married woman must cover her hair – a 'loose' woman (i.e. one wearing her hair loose and uncovered) is of easy virtue and up to no good. The only exceptions are a 'Queen in her splendour', or a bride on her wedding day.

An excess of wool production led to an Act of Parliament in 1571, in the reign of Queen Elizabeth, to boost the sales of English woollen cloth. It becomes law that on Sundays and every official holiday all males over 6 years of age, except for the nobility and persons of degree, are to wear woollen caps on pain of a fine of three farthings (¾ of a penny) per day. Whether it works or not in practice, the act is repealed in 1597. In June 1574, Elizabeth issues the following statute from Greenwich Palace:

> The excess of apparel and the superfluity of unnecessary foreign wares thereto belonging ... is grown to such an extremity that the decay of the whole realm is like to follow (by bringing into the realm such superfluities of silks, cloth of gold, silver, and other vain devices of so great cost as of necessity the moneys of the realm is yearly conveyed out of the same to answer the said excess) but also the undoing of a great number of young gentlemen seeking by show of apparel to be esteemed as gentlemen not only consume themselves, their goods, and lands which their parents left unto

them, but also run into such debts as they cannot live out of danger of laws without attempting unlawful acts ... [edited]

Despite the fact that the queen and everyone else understand the cost of trying to keep up with the latest fashions, no amount of law-making can prevent the young gallants from spending far beyond their means.

Another 1597 proclamation on the subject goes into minute detail. Only earls and upwards can wear cloth of gold or purple silk. No one under the degree of knight is allowed silk 'netherstocks' (long stockings) or velvet outer garments. A knight's eldest son may wear velvet doublets and hose but his younger brothers can't. A baron's eldest son's wife may wear gold or silver lace which is forbidden to women below her in the pecking order. Who is allowed to wear what is supposed to be strictly controlled as it's essential that the queen's subjects know their place and dress accordingly, so that no one can be misled. At least, that's the theory but you can see that the laws are confusing and is it any wonder that people ignore them? Will you obey the law or wear fashionable clothes, no matter the cost?

The frequency of acts and the huge number of laws passed proves that the authorities are losing the fight to keep the social distinctions, to maintain morals and ethics, preserve the English economy against foreign imports and restrain the excesses of fashion. However, a good many of the various sumptuary laws, dating back to as early as the fourteenth century, were still on the English statute books as recently as the 1800s and, who knows, some may as yet remain, hidden in the dusty archives in the twenty-first century.

Chapter 7

Home and Family

Home and family are as important to people in the sixteenth century as to us in the twenty-first. Marriage and children are what most of us hope and plan for in some form or another, unless you're a celibate priest, monk or nun. We like to think our name will carry on after we're gone, that our children's lives will be happy and successful. And the Tudors are no different.

What is the London Borough of Hackney in the twenty-first century, is in Tudor times a village in the countryside, three miles from the filth of the city and renowned for its 'healthful air', so it's a popular place where the wealthy build their country mansions. Thomas Cromwell has a mansion in nearby Clapton [Clopton in those days] and his one-time secretary, Ralph Sadleir, is busy constructing a grand three-storey house of brick in Hackney. Brick is still a novelty in England, rare enough that calling Ralph's mansion 'The Brick Place' is sufficient as an address – no other brick buildings stand in the area. Ralph's father, Henry, bought the site with the cash he'd made, helping to organise and equip Henry VIII's stupendous Field of the Cloth of Gold meeting with the King of France in 1520, being appointed as 'purveyor of all the buckram and canvas' required. Since the entire temporary landscape of palaces, pavilions and banqueting halls was constructed from these textiles, Henry Sadleir was well rewarded.

Young Ralph is Cromwell's secretary and in 1533 he marries his master's cousin, Helen (or Ellen) Barre. She lives in Cromwell's home in Fenchurch Street, taken in as a destitute woman, abandoned by her husband and left with two small daughters. With her first husband thought to have died in Ireland, Ralph and Helen are wed and come to live at Brick Place. Later that year their son, Thomas, is baptised in St Augustine's Church in Hackney with Cromwell standing as 'gossip' (the medieval/Tudor word for a godparent).

By now, Ralph is working directly for the king as his principal secretary, being involved in the Dissolution of the Monasteries and going on diplomatic missions to Scotland and France, receiving a knighthood and serving as a Privy Counsellor to both Henry VIII and later to Edward VI. But then, in October 1545, Ralph has to rush back to London to deal with a shocking family crisis. Let's ask him about it:

'Good day to you, Sir Ralph…'

'Good! I don't know about that. It's a disaster.'

'Well, thank you for inviting me to your lovely home. Oak panelling, glazed windows – such comfort is impressive. But tell us about your disaster, sir.'

'It's unbelievable, I tell you. Helen and I have been blissfully married for eleven years – notwithstanding the occasional misunderstanding that every man and his wife will have – and with seven fine children to prove the success of our union. We'll not mention young Tom's misdemeanours…'

'So what has happened to upset your happy marriage?'

'No doubt you know that Helen's first husband, Matthew Barre – the very devil himself – ran off to Ireland, abandoning her and their daughters, casting them upon Lord Cromwell's charity, she being his cousin. Helen made enquiries of him in Dunmow in Essex where they dwelt and visited his family at Sevenoaks in Kent but he couldn't be traced. It was our honest belief that the wretch was dead and Helen a widow before we wed. And now, like a lightning bolt out of a clear sky, who should appear in London but the 'long-dead' rascal, Matthew Barre! As a man of influence, I can't have my reputation tarnished as an adulterer and my wife a bigamist, can I?'

'Indeed not Sir Ralph. No wonder you were shocked.'

'Shocked? That's not the worst of it. An enquiry was held and Matthew's claim to be Helen's right and lawful husband was upheld. This is a terrible blow. It makes me out an adulterer and our children illegitimate – hardly good for my standing at court.'

'What will you do?'

'Maybe I should pay an assassin to run this wretch Barre through with a blunt blade for the trouble and distress he has caused. But no. The only way out of this difficulty is to pay for an Act of Parliament, annulling Helen's marriage to him, as though it had never happened, but this is an expensive business. Fortunately, the King's Grace has promised me £200, though I know not when it will be paid – in his will, perhaps, but I'll speak no more for 'tis treason to even mention the possibility of King Henry's, er, passing. Shhh.'

'Thank you for your honesty, sir. I wish you good luck in getting your promised £200.'[1]

Ralph's fine house has the modern convenience of an indoor privy in the master bedchamber and yet the only access to the upstairs rooms is by means of steps little better than a ladder – quite medieval.[2]

Ralph Sadleir by Hans Holbein, 1535.

Henry VIII – a much-married monarch

If you are interested in the Tudor period – as I'm sure you must be, since you are planning to travel there to experience life in sixteenth-century England for yourself – the one thing you must have heard about is the fact the Henry VIII had six wives. He's famous for it. And you probably know the rhyme that helps you to remember their fates:

> Divorced, beheaded, died.
> Divorced, beheaded, survived.

Just to remind you: Katherine of Aragon is Henry's first wife, loyal and loving for twenty years. She rules as regent in his absence abroad and is the perfect queen consort in every way but one: although she gives birth to a healthy daughter, Mary, she fails to produce a living male heir to continue the Tudor dynasty.

Wife number two is the famous Anne Boleyn. Henry becomes besotted with Anne just as Katherine reaches the age of being past child-bearing. He realises his only chance of having a male heir is to take a new, younger wife and vivacious Anne seems the perfect choice. He needs to divorce Katherine and decides the fact that she was previously briefly wedded to his elder brother, Arthur, before the latter died, makes her marriage to Henry invalid, despite two decades of living in harmony as man and wife. The Pope refuses to grant the divorce, giving rise to the king's 'Great Matter' (see Chapter 4). In the end, Henry changes the situation drastically, so he can grant himself a divorce and he marries Anne.

Queen Anne soon produces a child but it's another daughter, Elizabeth. A subsequent pregnancy – or two – at least one of which was a boy child, ends in miscarriage. Having argued that God was on his side during the divorce proceeding, knowing his great need of a male heir, Henry now decides God isn't on his side, otherwise Anne wouldn't have miscarried. The love between them – or lust in the king's case – has cooled anyway. Anne must go; but how? Another divorce? Not this time. Henry's solution is far more drastic.

Anne behaves in an unqueenly fashion, flirting with other men. Quite how far this goes, we can't be certain, but rumours are hot at court, linking her inappropriately with a humble minstrel, some of the king's closest body servants and even Anne's own brother, George Boleyn, Viscount Rochford. As the king's wife, sex with someone else is an act of treason because any resulting child must be of undoubted parentage as it may be the next ruling monarch. Anne and her admirers are accused of adultery, treason, and in George's case, incest. All are tried, found guilty and condemned to death. Sentences are carried out soon after and Anne is the last to die. She begs to be allowed to die by the sword, not by the headsman's blunt axe, and Henry permits an experienced executioner to come from St Omer to do the job. Let's ask him about it:

Monsieur Rombaud, welcome to England. What do you think of our great Tower of London? Magnificent, isn't it?'

'Pah. There are more impressive places in France and the Netherlands. I have lived and demonstrated my skills in both, as my father and grandfather and his father did before me. And all of us known as Jean Rombaud. We are a famous family of executioners, going back centuries but, biensûr, I am the most famous of all.'

'Why is that, monsieur?'

'Sacré bleu! You have not heard of my stupendous feats of skill, strength and dexterity? Parce que, I lately beheaded two felons together with but a single stroke of my sword.'

'Is that possible?'

'Biensûr. Shall I demonstrate? I have my sword to hand here, ready honed to the sharpest edge.'

'Er no. I believe you, monsieur. It's a monstrous weapon, indeed. It must be of such a weight. Are you being well paid for this onerous task?'

'Comme ci; comme ça. You know how it is with you English, reluctant to pay for the best.'

'I hear you are to receive £23 plus expenses. That seems generous to me just for one sword cut.'

'But it is the most merciful means of dispatch in the hands of a master such as me. The client has no need to put their head on a wood block – so undignified. They may stand or kneel, as they wish, though I advise kneeling: the body has not so far to fall, so appears more elegant in death. Also, I guarantee to take but a solitary stroke to sever the head from the neck, whereas you inept English with your blunted axes can take numerous attempts, chopping and hacking. Comme c'est sauvage! No wonder your queen requested my services.'

'Monsieur Rombaud, you will make it quick this morning for Anne, won't you?'

'Ah. You have, as you English say, a soft spot for her. Oui?'

'Maybe.'

'You should hold your tongue, if you are wise. Le Roi Henri might learn of your sympathies and you will be the next to feel my blade.'

'But there, I see the queen's little procession approaching. I shall leave you to your grisly work, monsieur. See how graceful and dignified she is, as though she goes to a second coronation: so brave of step and head held high.'

'Not for much longer, English fool. I bid you "adieu". Or perhaps "au revoir", until you are in need of my skills.'

'Never, monsieur. I intend to keep my head exactly where it is, firmly upon my shoulders.'

'Les temps ou le Roi, will tell.

A few days before Anne Boleyn is executed for having committed treason by means of adultery, Henry's marriage to her was declared officially null and void. Which raises an interesting question: since this declaration means the couple had NEVER been legally wed, how can Anne be guilty of treason or adultery, even if she has had sex with other men?

Wife number three is Jane Seymour who has the advantage that both her predecessors are dead – Katherine of natural causes; Anne by the swordsman's blade. Thus, Henry is a widower so there can be no doubt this marriage is legal – a fact supported in Henry's eyes in that God finally grants him the longed for male heir necessary to continue the Tudor dynasty. Jane's triumph is brief though because she dies of childbirth complications when the baby, Prince Edward, is not yet two weeks old. However, Henry celebrates her as his one true

Imaginary family portrait of Henry VIII with his deceased wife, Jane Seymour, and her son, Prince Edward, c.1543–47.

wife and has a family portrait painted which includes her and young Edward as though she had lived. When he dies, the king is buried beside Jane in St George's Chapel at Windsor Castle.

Once more a widower, Henry mourns Jane for a while but, realising that having only one son leaves the dynasty vulnerable – having 'an heir and a spare' is always advisable, after all, he was once 'the spare' – the king decides to take a fourth wife. Anne of Cleves, a German Protestant princess, is his choice, based not only on her attractive looks, according to both her portrait and diplomatic reports, but her family will be his much-needed Protestant allies. But, whatever her personal and political assets, Henry cannot take to his latest bride and their union ends in a swift divorce. Anne is treated well and honourably as 'the king's sister'. Henry sends her gifts occasionally and she lives quietly, sometimes at Richmond Palace and also at Anne Boleyn's family home, Hever Castle in Kent. She outlives the king by ten years and is buried in queenly state in Westminster Abbey.

Wife number five is young enough to be Henry's daughter, though her exact age isn't certain. Katherine Howard is a lively, attractive teenager pushed before the ageing king by her powerful, scheming uncle, Thomas Howard, the 3rd Duke of Norfolk. Henry is smitten, no doubt yearning for his own lost youth. But Katherine is naïve and has no experience of courtly intrigue. Her uncle's numerous enemies see ways to undermine his power by destroying his niece. Poor Katherine makes it easy for them, flirting with her previous boyfriend, Thomas Culpepper, at court. She's too young to have learned from the fate of her cousin, Anne Boleyn, a decade before. Henry is reluctant to believe the rumours but, eventually, is convinced by Howard's enemies that his queen is committing adultery. Katherine's end is inevitable and she isn't granted the mercy of a French swordsman. She is executed on Tower Green like Anne Boleyn, but by the headman's axe. Both cousins are buried in the chapel of St Peter ad Vincula within the Tower of London.

By now, Henry can deny his age no longer. Always a bit of a hypochondriac, the incapacitating ulcers on his leg and his resulting excess weight are all too real. For wife number six, he wants a more mature woman to comfort him and nurse him through his various ailments. Alone among his queens, his next choice, Katherine Parr, has been married before – twice – and had to nurse both husbands through their final sickness. Still pretty at 30 years of age, she would seem to be ideal despite the fact she is already in love with, and planning to wed, Thomas Seymour, brother of Queen Jane. The couple's wedding has to be put on hold when the king chooses Katherine as his sixth and last queen.

Like her most recent predecessor, Katherine Parr isn't an experienced courtier but she learns quickly. She and the king share spirited discussions on matters of religion and her opponents try to convince Henry that she's undermining his new Church of England by her more extreme Protestantism. But clever Katherine flatters her husband, telling him she is only trying to learn from his vastly superior wisdom and knowledge. She's patient and caring towards him and manages to persuade him to bring his two daughters, Mary and Elizabeth, back to court, so they can be one big happy family together again before his death.

When Henry VIII dies in January 1547, Katherine returns to her lover, Thomas Seymour. The couple marry and Katherine soon conceives her first child. Her daughter, Mary, is born at Sudeley Castle in Gloucestershire but Katherine dies soon after of complications and is buried in the castle chapel.

So ends the saga of King Henry's ill-fated six queens. I think Anne of Cleves is the most fortunate of his wives. As a time-traveller, my advice to you is do all you can to avoid marrying a king – or a queen, for that matter.

Childbirth – 'To be or not to be?'

As you will have realised by now, childbirth is fraught with danger, even for queens who must surely receive the best medical treatment available, so my best advice to any female time-traveller is to avoid pregnancy at all costs, if you want to survive your visit to Tudor England. One method would be to follow Queen Elizabeth's example and remain a virgin, although even in her case there are rumours to the contrary and vague suggestions that she'd had a baby, but don't spread this gossip or childbirth will be the least of your worries.

However, some women seem to survive repeated pregnancies without too many problems or heartbreak. While Henry VIII only produced three legitimate children from six marriages, Thomas Howard, 2nd Duke of Norfolk, victor at the battle of Flodden in 1513, only marries twice yet sires eight sons and two daughters by his first wife and three sons and four daughters by his second. The king must be so envious. Thomas's third son by his first wife is Edmund Howard. Described as a lazy fellow in general, yet he's no slouch in the bedchamber. By his first wife, Joyce Culpepper – a widow who has already had two sons and three daughters – Edmund fathers three more sons and three more daughters, one of whom, Katherine, becomes King Henry's fifth wife. Apparently, the sexy teenager manages to revive the old king's flagging libido – yet another heir does not result. Is this Henry's failure? Possibly. After all Katherine's mother seems fertile enough and the Howards certainly are, so why shouldn't Katherine conceive? There may be another reason.

Despite her youth, Katherine had definitely had sex with at least two men without getting pregnant before she married the king. In fact, she seems pretty certain that isn't going to happen unless she wishes it and is believed to have said that 'a woman might meddle with a man and yet conceive no child unless she would herself.'[3] Unfortunately she doesn't elaborate on which method of birth control she relies on – or is it just some old wives' tale and she happens to be lucky? Such things aren't discussed because contraception is illegal in Tudor England which is why we know little about it, since nobody dared put such things in writing. The Church, of whatever religious persuasion, regards sex as being for the procreation of children and no other reason, so having a good time without the intention of getting pregnant is absolutely forbidden. However, the Church has to admit that sex for the fun of it is going to happen, so a few methods of avoiding conception are tolerated. Saying 'no' is permitted and also the most reliable, unless you're a wife, in which case it's your marital duty to say 'yes', whether you're in the mood or not, unless you're already pregnant or breast-feeding. Physical methods, such as keeping sexual exploits to the woman's less fertile times, is even less effective in the Tudor era than in the twenty-first century because it's believed she is most likely to conceive just before and just after her period, so the middle of the month is thought the safest – which we know is the exact opposite. Maybe you can enlighten them? The withdrawal method, requiring so much self-control by the man, is disgusting in the eyes of the Church as a waste of 'precious seed', as is male masturbation. As for women's self-enjoyment, the Church refuses to believe that ever happens and although the Tudors are the first to make homosexuality a crime in England, the laws don't apply to women because there are no such things as lesbians! The Tudor law-makers – all male, of course – can't imagine women having a good time without men.

As far as we know, condoms aren't around in Tudor England, although animal intestines are used as sheaths in parts of Europe in the next century. If you have the opportunity, you could introduce the idea here first, especially as venereal diseases (and syphilis in particular) are becoming more prevalent. However, women are known to use 'barriers', inserting vinegar-soaked wool, little rolls of linen or silk-sponges. These last are natural sponges, imported from the Mediterranean, which become soft and silky in texture when wet and very absorbent. Beeswax is also used to block the path of the man's semen and one source I read says pebbles and pieces of wood are also tried – but they sound too painful.

More like witchcraft, some Tudor women still put their trust in ancient charms and folklore – I suppose, if you're desperate, you'll try anything. Wearing amulets made from the appropriate parts of male animals, weasel testicles being popular, is believed to make the 'atmosphere' of the woman's body more masculine and, therefore, less likely to conceive. But the most suspect method is using various herbal remedies which bears a definite taint of witchcraft and is doubly dangerous although probably the most effective method of contraception. Any woman supplying such remedies can be charged with being a witch and burned at the stake and her customers reckoned as murderers of their unconceived or unborn children. And then there are the dangers of taking the herbs themselves. Herbs such as rue and pennyroyal are prescribed to 'bring down a woman's menses or flowers', i.e. bring on her period, so preventing a fertilised egg from implanting in the womb. Otherwise, if the woman is already pregnant, these herbs can cause the foetus to abort, resulting in miscarriage.

This brings us to another difficulty for the female time-traveller: if your chosen method of contraception is successful, how do you

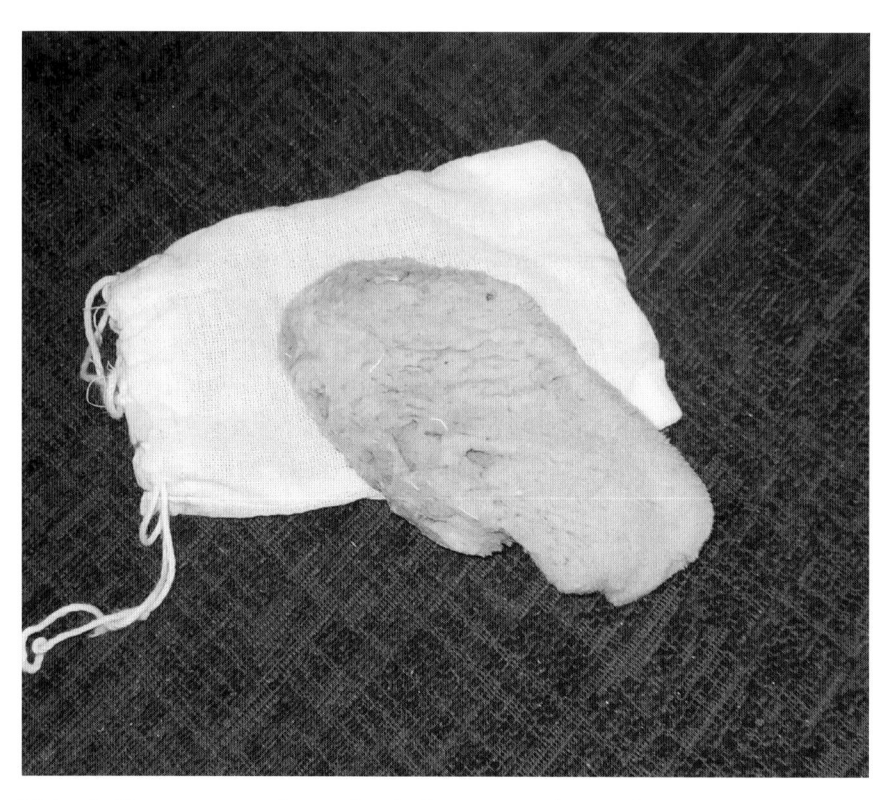

Natural silk-sponges can be used as both contraceptives and tampons.

cope with the result – having monthly periods? The silk-sponges mentioned above can also be used, trimmed and shaped to a suitable size with a cord attached, as washable, reusable tampons.[4]

However, it seems that most Tudor women, queens included, use absorbent linen napkins or rags as their sanitary products – a method that continued into the twentieth century. These are washed out and saved for next month, but how are they kept safely in position? Well, if women do indeed wear knickers those will help and surprisingly, Queen Elizabeth's household accounts hold another clue. Along with listing dozens of 'vallopes' of fine Holland cloth – a soft linen – of various lengths there are three 'gyrdelles' of black silk with buckles and hooks and eyes 'whipped' with silk so they wouldn't chafe.[5] 'Vallopes' or wallops are loose rags, so the longer ones are likely to be folded into a thick pad for use as sanitary towels and the shorter ones rolled into tampons. The towels can be hooked onto the girdles which are 'made on the fingers' i.e. by finger-weaving which makes a narrow braided ribbon.

Royal husbands and wannabes

We have considered the perils of being a royal wife – something to be avoided at all costs – but what if a queen is in need of a husband? What are your chances and what are the pitfalls? Firstly, I suggest you avoid marrying a woman who is even remotely a possible contender for the throne. When Lady Jane Grey is pushed onto the throne by her Dudley in-laws in 1556 it doesn't end well for her or her young husband, Guilford Dudley. In just nine dramatic summer days, Guilford goes from king-in-all-but-name – England had never had a ruling queen before so her husband was expected to take charge, even if Jane thought otherwise – to a candidate for the executioner. And it's on the block that Guilford's short career ends. He hadn't married a queen but he died along with one.

Jane is swiftly replaced as queen by Henry VIII's elder daughter, Mary, who is already 37 years old and hasn't got a husband, so the race is on to find a suitable spouse and produce the required heir as soon as possible. As a queen-regnant i.e. one who rules in her own right as opposed to a queen-consort who is just the king's wife, Mary's choice of bachelors who are of similar rank is very limited. Protestant suitors need not apply because Mary intends to return England to the Roman Catholic Church. Anyone of less than royal birth is out of the question. Since unwed Catholic kings are few, Mary chooses the only likely candidate: her cousin Philip, heir to the Spanish throne and the vast Habsburg Empire. Philip is only 26 and Mary is a bit old to be a blushing bride but the lure of being King of England even before he becomes King of Spain is irresistible, especially as Mary seems to be willing to let him 'wear the trousers' – or the galligaskins, at least.

The couple marry in Winchester Cathedral on 25 July 1554, just a year after Mary becomes queen and only two days after their first meeting. The trouble is that Parliament wanted her to marry an Englishman and Philip is an unpopular foreigner. Although Parliament insists that Philip isn't allowed to drag England into Spanish wars and politics, he is recognised as co-monarch and everything from coinage to state papers and summonses to Parliament must bear the names of both Philip and Mary. All state papers have to be copied into Latin or Spanish because the new king doesn't speak a word of English.

Sadly for Mary, her marriage doesn't produce an heir – although wishful thinking seems to have caused a phantom pregnancy. When she dies in November 1558, Philip loses his English crown but since he is now a widower and Mary is succeeded by her unmarried half-sister Elizabeth, he reckons he has a good chance of regaining it by marrying Elizabeth and she's a younger, more attractive prospect as a wife. In fact, he had been viewed as a possible husband for Elizabeth back in Henry VIII's reign but this time he has numerous competitors. In the first year of her reign, proposals of marriage flood in from Englishmen including Sir William Pickering; James Hamilton, Earl of Arran; Henry FitzAlan, Earl of Arundel and Lord Robert Dudley.[6] Most of these men are just fortune hunters and Elizabeth doesn't take them serious, except for one: Robert Dudley.

Home and Family

Robert, as Queen Jane Grey's brother-in-law, had been imprisoned in the Tower of London by Mary. No doubt he half-expected to follow his brother Guilford to the scaffold. Princess Elizabeth was also a prisoner there at the same time because Mary didn't trust her and she, like Robert, feared life would be short. It seems likely their shared fears and misfortunes brought Robert and Elizabeth together.

Now Elizabeth is queen, Robert may be the perfect spouse: handsome, noble for a couple of generations – his grandfather, Edmund, had been one of Henry VII's loathed tax-gatherers, executed for his efforts – and definitely English and so preferred by the queen's subjects. Within days of her taking the throne, Robert is given the plum post as her Master of Horse. He becomes a Privy Counsellor, a Knight of the Order of the Garter and Lord Steward of the Royal Household and, in 1564, is ennobled as Earl of Leicester. But there is one difficulty: Robert already has a wife, Amy Robsart, whom he

Robert Dudley, Earl of Leicester.

married in 1550 and it's said to have been a love match. However, the possibility of a crown is tempting.

In 1560, more illustrious foreign suitors send their ambassadors to the English court to woo Elizabeth: King Eric XVI of Sweden; the Duke of Holstein; King Charles IX of France and Henry de Valois, Duke of Anjou. Offers from each are encouraged one day and rejected the next. Elizabeth keeps them all vying for her favour without promising them anything in return but Robert is always conspicuous at her side. Amy Dudley, though, is never seen at court, having to make do with infrequent short visits from her husband.

And then, in September 1560, Robert's wife dies, falling down stairs and breaking her neck. A coroner's inquest concludes her death is an accident, but it's too convenient and rumours of murder flourish. Robert and the queen are at Windsor together when it happens but gossip implies their involvement in planning Amy's demise. To avoid embarrassment, Elizabeth has no choice but to send her beloved Robert away from court for a while until the rumours fade, but she knows she can never wed a man suspected, however remotely, of killing his wife.

Robert, though, doesn't give up his quest and why should he when, after a brief interlude, the queen continues to shower him with favours, including an earldom and vast estates in the Midlands, including Kenilworth Castle in Warwickshire. It's here that he entertains Elizabeth in 1575, spending lavishly on state rooms, food, entertainments and redesigning the gardens for an exceptional nineteen-day visit. Let's talk to Robert about his preparations:

> 'My Lord Robert, with Her Majesty arriving tomorrow, can you tell us a little of what you have planned for her visit?'
>
> 'I'm so busy but I suppose I can do no more now. As you'll see, I've constructed a bridge 600ft in length so the queen may ride her horse across the lake – from which the Lady of the Lake will arise – and I've built a new gate house to impress her when she arrives at the castle.'

'No doubt you've redecorated a bedchamber especially for her?'

'A bedchamber! I've built an entire new house of sumptuous private apartments for us – er, I mean for the queen and her close servants. It has its own dancing chamber as Her Majesty loves to dance. Dancing *la volta* with me whenever… But what do you think of the new garden, eh? Splendid, isn't it? Note the jewelled aviary among the fruit trees and fragrant flowers. I've imported song birds from far and wide to fill the aviary with melody.'

'Very lovely. What else do you have planned – nineteen days of listening to birds chirping isn't all that exciting, is it?'

'You're no better than a philistine, are you? Well for your kind, there will be hunting, bear-baitings, Italian acrobats, boating on the lake, jousting, mock battles and ceremonial cannonades. Does that please you better?'

'I'm no brute, my lord. I enjoy the finer things too.'

'Then you'll approve the ambrosial banquet of 300 sweet dishes, as well as the feasts every day. There will be a huge ornamental dolphin to rise from the lake, pregnant with six musicians in its belly.'

'Is that to remind the queen that she still needs an heir?'

'Hush! There will also be something you'll never have seen before: fireworks made of gunpowder, including one which burns underwater. Such a novelty. There will be water pageants and plays. I have spared no expense.'

'Is this royal visit going to bankrupt you, Lord Robert?'

'Not quite but it's worth it if my Sovereign Lady will only grant me her gracious hand … oh, no … there's a disaster with one of the bears … must dash…'[7]

Poor Lord Robert never marries the queen. Instead, he weds an old flame, Lettice Knollys, the queen's cousin and when Elizabeth finds out she flies into a rage. That rage lasts five years before he is allowed to return to court. When Robert dies in 1588, the queen locks herself in her chamber to grieve. Days later, Lord Burghley has to order the door to be broken down. It's said that she emerges 'much aged and spent and very melancholy', so it seems Robert Dudley was her one true love.

Therefore, although Lord Robert doesn't meet his end on the block, if you want to survive, unscathed in Tudor England, my advice is don't so much as contemplate marrying the monarch.

Chapter 8

Surviving at the Royal Court

Having avoided marrying anyone too royal to be safe, the monarch's court is still a dangerous place as Cardinal Wolsey and Thomas Cromwell will tell you. Falling from favour with the king can have unfortunate consequences, even if it doesn't end at the scaffold. But there are those who seem to have a knack for surviving. One such at the court of both Henry VII and Henry VIII is Richard Clement.[1]

Surviving fickle fortune

Sir Richard Clement begins his career early in the Tudor era and is first listed as a Page of the King's Privy Chamber to Henry VII when he attends the funeral of the king's wife, Queen Elizabeth of York in 1503. By the time he is noted as being at Henry VII's deathbed in 1509, Clement has been promoted to Groom of the Privy Chamber, one of the king's most intimate servants. He and the other Privy Chamber servants are required to keep the king's death a secret, carrying out their duties as if he were still alive for two days, until his son is publicly confirmed as Henry VIII. The new king uses those two days to arrest Edmund Dudley – grandfather of Robert, Earl of Leicester – and his fellow tax-gatherer, Richard Empson, before they learn that the old king they served so well is dead. Having Henry VII's detested tax officials executed is a popular beginning to the new reign. Meanwhile, Clement is supplied with mourning clothes to attend the old king's funeral before the new king dismisses all his father's intimate servants, replacing them with his own friends and favourites.

Ightham Mote in Kent, Richard Clement's country house.

But Richard Clement's career isn't finished. By 1513, he is a Gentleman Usher and takes an active part in the battle of the Spurs – an English victory in France. In 1521, he buys a nice manor house in the Kentish countryside, Ightham Mote (see Chapter 2). His new and influential neighbours are the Boleyns at Hever Castle, the Sidneys at Penshurst Place and the Archbishop of Canterbury at Knole.

In 1529, Clement receives a knighthood for helping his neighbour, William Wareham, the Archbishop of Canterbury, when 'a host of belligerent Kentishmen' attack the archbishop's palace at nearby Knole. Now Sir Richard Clement, he has other important neighbours not far away at Hever Castle: Thomas Boleyn, Earl of Wiltshire. Boleyn is Clement's patron and Sir Richard receives an invitation to the event of the year in 1533 when Boleyn's daughter, Anne, is crowned queen, as Henry VIII's second wife, in Westminster Abbey. It's a gorgeous and splendid spectacle.

In 1534, as Sheriff of Kent, Clement becomes involved in an argument over property between a local vicar and a servant of Sir Edward Guildford, another neighbour. Clement surrounds Guildford's house with 200 men, demanding that the servant is handed over for trial. A rude response ends in shots being exchanged before Clement has the servant dragged out and taken to gaol. Guildford makes an official complaint, stating that Clement has overstepped his authority. Clement is summoned to appear in the Court of Star Chamber, found guilty and committed to the Fleet Prison in London. Is this the end of Clement's career?

No, because Sir Thomas Boleyn, Anne's father, pleads his case and Clement is shortly released. But to be a survivor in Tudor times, you have to be prepared to change sides. When Anne Boleyn's triumph doesn't last, Clement is fortunate that he isn't too closely associated with Anne and manages to keep his head, unlike some others of her friends. The Boleyns' timely support when he was imprisoned doesn't prevent Clement becoming involved in the trial and downfall of Queen Anne just two years later. To keep in the king's favour, in May 1536, Clement sits on the Grand Jury of Kent, held at Deptford, to consider and rule on the alleged crimes of the queen. Clement continues to investigate crimes in Kent, from tax-evasion to manslaughter, until his death from natural causes in 1538.

Sir Richard Clement is a Tudor survivor and I advise you to take note of his methods: make friends with influential people but be ready to abandon them in a hurry, if the situation requires such drastic action.

Surviving the plague

There is no way to guarantee you'll survive the plague, if you're unfortunate enough to catch it, so the best thing is to avoid it. Henry VIII, always paranoid about disease of any kind, goes to extreme lengths in the winter of 1525 when there are cases of plague in London and across southern England. He withdraws to the relative safety of Eltham Palace, downriver from London, with a much-reduced court, far fewer servants and nobody is allowed to leave or visit the palace. Christmas is going to be a minimal affair this year.

Meanwhile, Cardinal Wolsey, showing contempt for the plague – if not for the king's paranoia – keeps Christmas in fine style at Richmond Palace, upriver from London. As Edward Hall writes in his *Chronicle* 'the Cardinal … kept open household to lords, ladies and all others that would come, with plays and disguisings in [a] most royal manner'. Wolsey is at the peak of his power and utterly disregards the king's rulings put in place to protect the court from the plague. Instead, he puts on lavish celebrations, just as he wishes, and Hall notes that Henry's servants, forced to suffer a miserable Christmas at Eltham, are 'sore grieved'. As for the king, Hall doesn't tell us of his reaction but we can guess he was probably furious at his orders being ignored and the cardinal's blatant display of disrespect.

It's little wonder that Henry's servants are fed up because Christmas at the Tudor court is usually spectacular with the celebrations going on from Christmas Eve until Epiphany on the 6 January. Playing (and gambling) at cards, dice and other games of chance, officially prohibited at court for the rest of the year, are allowed during the Twelve Days of Christmas. Entertainments include masques (disguisings) and dramas, dancing, musical interludes, hunting and jousting. And, of course, huge feasts of forty or more dishes, served in four courses twice a day, at 10 am and 4 pm, with the banquet of sweetmeats to follow. Missing all that food and merriment is bound to upset everyone – as we know in the UK, since Christmas 2020 was cancelled due to the Covid-19 lockdown.

And this is Hall's description of the pageant in the Great Hall at Richmond Palace during a previous Christmas, giving an idea of the scale and spectacle of the celebrations:

> Before the banquet … was a pageant [performed with a set that looked] like a mountain glittering by night, as

though it had been [made] all of gold and set with stones, on the top of the which mountain was a tree of gold, the branches and boughs [trimmed] with gold, spreading over the mountain with roses and pomegranates [the badges of Henry VIII and Katherine of Aragon] … and out of the mountain came a lady [wearing] cloth of gold, and children of honour called the Henchmen, who were freshly disguised, and [they] danced a Morris before the King. And that done [they] re-entered the mountain and then it was drawn back, and then was the wassail or banquet brought in.[2]

Christmas at Eltham isn't much fun compared to that.

Secret agents and assassins

Her father was paranoid about disease but Elizabeth and her ministers are more concerned about Catholic agencies plotting to kill the Protestant queen. Early in her reign, William Cecil, Lord Burghley, sets up a network of agents to sniff out any plots aimed at her majesty but as her chief minister, sometime Secretary of State and Lord High Treasurer, he has so much other business to fill his time, the gathering of intelligence is put in the capable hands of Francis Walsingham.

In 1568, the threat of plots increases when Mary, Queen of Scots, Elizabeth's Catholic cousin with a valid claim of her own to the English throne, crosses the border into England. Mary has fled from her rebellious Scottish subjects and comes to beg her cousin's assistance to put them in their place so she can return to rule Scotland. However, it shocks everyone: Scots, English and Europeans, when instead of treating her as a royal cousin and fellow queen, Elizabeth has Mary taken under guard as a prisoner. For the next nineteen years, Mary tries to gain an audience with Elizabeth but the two never meet and the Scots' queen spends all that time as a prisoner, moved from castle to castle, around England.

Lord Burghley's spies begin uncovering plots almost straightaway as Mary is a magnet for disgruntled Catholics wanting to put her on the throne in place of Elizabeth. In 1569, there is an uprising in the North of England, led by the Catholic Earls of Westmorland and Northumberland, trying to do exactly this but it ends in disaster for the rebels. The Ridolfi plot in 1571 has similar aims but is uncovered just in time. However, the increasing danger to Elizabeth is obvious and Burghley brings in Francis Walsingham as the queen's spy-master.

In 1570 (as we saw in Chapter 4) Pope Pius V in Rome adds to the difficulties by issuing a papal bull: a directive to all Roman Catholics that Elizabeth, Queen of England, has been excommunicated by the Catholic Church. This bull relieves Catholics of their obligation to recognise her sovereignty as God's anointed. Her Catholic subjects can abandon any pretence of loyalty to her and Catholic monarchs across Europe are not only encouraged, but should feel obliged, to remove her from power and bring England back to the Roman Church.

Walsingham, strongly Protestant, quick-witted and ruthless, is the ideal man to uncover any devious Catholic schemes threatening the queen and the country. He was born at his uncle Edmund's house, Scadbury Manor at Chislehurst in Kent, probably in 1532. His father, a lawyer named William, had served Henry VIII, carrying out the investigations into Cardinal Wolsey's affairs, leading to the churchman's downfall, but died when his son was a toddler.

Francis Walsingham sets up an intelligence network at home and abroad to keep him informed about what English Catholics are up to, the attitudes of foreign countries to England and the Pope's policies towards Elizabeth. By intercepting letters across Europe and in England, he learns the identity of Catholic dissidents and keeps track of their intrigues.

Spies have to be clever and Walsingham recruits undergraduates from Oxford and Cambridge – just as the Soviet Union did in the twentieth century. But spying isn't as romantic as James Bond makes

Ruins of Scadbury Manor, Chislehurst, Kent, birthplace of Francis Walsingham.

out. Mostly, it's poorly paid – if you get paid at all when the boss remembers you – and involves a lot of arduous travelling and living in less than comfortable circumstances. It's often boring and repetitive and, of course, can be extremely dangerous if you get caught.

Do you enjoy solving puzzles and like taking risks? Then Walsingham's spy school may be just the place to begin a new career. There, you will learn how to break the plotters' numerous methods of encoding their correspondence and how to encrypt your own secret messages. Using milk, lemon juice or onion juice as invisible ink is one simple method, although sending a blank paper with a definite smell might be suspicious, so I suggest you incorporate the secret bits within a letter about innocent matters written in normal ink. Warming the page makes the invisible ink appear. Some codes shuffle the alphabet in a particular sequence and a key word must be known in order to unravel that sequence. This should test your puzzle-solving skills. Or individual letters can be replaced with numbers, symbols or

> **Did You Know?**
>
> Some codes require a sheet of paper punched with holes laid over the top of a page so that just the relevant letters making up the message can be read. Success depends on the exact sequence of thousands of holes. I've seen this method used on a specified page of the Bible but both sender and recipient must have identical printed copies of the book.

signs of the zodiac, though this isn't likely to be as straightforward as A=1, B=2, C=3, etc.

In 1583, Walsingham's spies discover a dangerous plot which involves not only Mary, Queen of Scots, but both the French and Spanish ambassadors, using a young Catholic Englishman, Francis Throckmorton, as go-between. The plan is for a French invasion, with financial backing from both Philip II of Spain and the Pope, to overthrow Elizabeth and put Mary in her place. But Throckmorton's frequent meetings with the Spanish ambassador Mendoza arouse suspicion and Walsingham has the young Catholic watched. Eventually, Throckmorton is arrested and his house searched. Among the incriminating letters found there are details of the planned French invasion. Under torture, Throckmorton admits his part in the treasonous scheme but insists it isn't progressing because King Philip's cash contribution hasn't materialised. Nevertheless, he is tried, convicted and executed for treason in 1584.

Although the plot is a failure, Mendoza is expelled from England and relationships with both France and Spain deteriorate. The queen and her government, desperate to keep her safe from enemies at home and abroad, devise the Bond of Association to be signed by everyone of significance in the land, agreeing that any plotters against the queen will receive the death penalty without exception. Both Lord Burghley and Walsingham try to convince Elizabeth that, according to the terms of the bond, Mary should be executed but Elizabeth refuses to admit the evidence against her cousin.

Sir Francis Walsingham by John de Critz the Elder.

In 1586, Walsingham's spies uncover another dangerous plot to assassinate Elizabeth, involving a group of young English Catholics led by Anthony Babington. By this time, Mary has been a prisoner for almost twenty years, always the centre of intrigue, corresponding with the plotters, and Walsingham has come to hate the Scots' Queen. This is his chance to be rid of her at long last with a carefully staged plan – more devious than anything the Catholics can devise.

First, Walsingham plants a double agent, Gifford, working for the brewer who supplies Mary with beer. Regularly delivering full barrels and taking away the empties, Gifford makes certain he is the queen's ideal contact with the outside world, unremarkable and almost unnoticed, smuggling letters in both directions. Written in a basic code, they are quickly deciphered by an expert, Thomas Philips, before being resealed and sent on. Copies in plain English are given to Elizabeth so she's aware of the unfolding plot. And it isn't just incriminating mail. Babington and his fellow conspirators have no idea of secrecy and chat about their plans in public, making it easy for Walsingham's spies to keep track of their whereabouts and what they're doing.

Second, we come to the crux of the plot for both Babington and Walsingham: now Mary is aware of the plans, will she agree to take part? Imagine Walsingham's delight when Gifford carries a letter from Mary, asking for the details of the rescue mission to release her from imprisonment with a view to her taking the English crown – an undoubted act of treason. He now has Mary in his trap – but he also wants the conspirators.

So third, Walsingham forges a post script to this letter, seemingly in Mary's handwriting, before forwarding it to Babington. The post script asks for the names of all the conspirators, presumably, so she can reward them all when the plot is successful. I imagine that Walsingham can hardly wait for Babington's reply to be deciphered and whoever decodes the list of names sketches a gallows at the bottom of the translation. Indeed, that will be the plotters' reward: every one of them drawn, hanged and quartered as a warning to others to keep well away from intrigue with the Queen of Scots.

Mary's fate is sealed but at her trial she tries to discredit Walsingham's evidence, insisting that 'spies make a show of one thing and speak another'. But then that's what spies are meant to do. She is found guilty, tried by Sir Ralph Sadleir and others as we saw earlier, and sentenced to death on 4 December 1586. But the job isn't done yet. Elizabeth still has to be persuaded to sign the death warrant. Putting a fellow monarch – God's anointed – to death is not a step

Did You Know?

Scottish monarchs only rule their people – the Scots. They do not own the land of Scotland as the English monarch owns England. Hence, they are King or Queen of Scots, not of Scotland.

Mary, Queen of Scots, as a young woman by François Clouet.

to be taken lightly. After all, it may set a precedent that others might decide to follow, if you're ever in a similar situation. And, of course, she's Elizabeth's cousin, even if they have never met.

Elizabeth does sign the death warrant but, even so, she drops huge hints that she'll be very pleased if somebody would oblige her and do away with Mary under the terms of the Bond of Association, so avoiding an official execution. Nobody volunteers but Burghley and the Privy Council send the warrant to Fotheringhay Castle, where Mary is held, without informing the queen so that she can deny all knowledge and – who knows? – just maybe she had intended to be merciful and revoke the warrant. We aren't fooled; it had to be done. Mary is beheaded in the hall of the castle on 8 February 1587. Unfortunately for Mary, it's a botched job and takes three attempts. Those who see it later claim that her lips continued to pray for fifteen minutes afterwards and when the executioner went to hold the head aloft, her wig came off in his hand and she was bald beneath it. So, be warned: the stress of plotting against Elizabeth can cause you to lose your hair even before you lose your head.

Francis Walsingham succeeds in keeping his, but with Mary dead his job is done. Elizabeth never really appreciates his loyalty to her, nor his hard work. She certainly doesn't pay for the spy network which Walsingham has been funding out of his own purse. The spy-master dies in 1590 but the work continues with Lord Burghley and his son, Robert Cecil, now in charge of the intelligence gathering.

A scapegoat?

Queen Elizabeth suffers headaches and, rumours suggest, female problems and other minor ailments. Even so, she lives to the age of 70. But, as you'd expect, to guard against illness, she has a sizable staff of medical practitioners with at least fifteen physicians and seven surgeons being paid £100 in board and receiving other perks, benefits and gifts. The queen prefers men who have studied at Oxford and Cambridge, but one exception is Dr Rodrigo Lopes from Portugal. Lopes was born into a Jewish family but they were forced to convert to Catholicism almost a century before. Lopes qualified as a physician in 1544 but he is suspected of continuing Jewish practices by the Portuguese Inquisition so he flees to England. Here, he joins the Church of England, being baptised, taking the name Roger.

Lopes practises at St Bartholomew's Hospital in London and becomes chief physician there in 1567. He is famed for the success of a remedy made to his own recipe of sumac and aniseed and becomes well known. His patients include Robert Dudley, Earl of Leicester, Francis Walsingham and, later, Robert Devereux, Earl of Essex.

In 1580, Philip II of Spain invades Portugal and England offers a home to any enemy of King Philip, including Dom Antonio, a bastard claimant to the throne of Portugal. Lopes acts as an intermediary between Burghley and Walsingham and the Portuguese refugees. Great as a spy, he speaks five languages and sets up a clandestine correspondence with the court of Spain, insisting that it's Walsingham's idea. He becomes Elizabeth's chief physician in 1586 and is soon granted the monopoly on importing his favourite medicinal ingredients, sumac and aniseed, into England.

The intrigue grows deeper. Known Portuguese agents live at Lopes' London home and their correspondence with the Spanish

Dr Roger Lopes (left) speaking to a Spaniard, an engraving by E. Hulsius.

ambassador in Spain is intercepted by Walsingham's spies. There is no firm evidence that Lopes is conspiring against the queen but things don't look good. Then, one night in 1593, the queen's current favourite, Robert Devereux, throws a party at his London residence, Essex House, and Dom Antonio, Roger Lopes and Philip II's disgraced former secretary, Antonio Perez, are guests. These three are chatting about their host and his sexual activities when Lopes lets slip the fact that Devereux, his patient, has syphilis. Later, Perez tells Devereux of this very personal breach of doctor-patient confidentiality. Devereux is livid and swears to take his revenge on Lopes.

By coincidence, Devereux has his own spy network and Lopes is providing intelligence to him as well as to Robert Cecil as the official queen's spy-master. This means Devereux has easy access to incriminating evidence to bring down Lopes. Letters are 'discovered' implicating Lopes in foreign plots. Lopes insists he is innocent and that the Cecils know of his plans to double-cross Spain by seeming to support their intrigues. When questioned, the Cecils believe him and the queen herself intervenes on her physician's behalf, telling Devereux that he is 'a rash and temerious youth, to enter into the matter against the poor man, which he could not prove, but whose innocence she knew well enough'.

Devereux is furious and refuses to give up his campaign against Lopes. He invents evidence that the physician was plotting to poison the queen. Two Portuguese agents are tortured into confirming the plot, admitting Lopes agreed to assassinate the queen by poisoning her and that Philip II of Spain was paying him 50,000 crowns. Fearing torture, Lopes confesses and although he later retracts his confession, the damage is done. He is tried at Guildhall in London on 28 February 1594 with Devereux testifying against him. Lopes maintains his innocence throughout but suddenly his Jewish heritage is held against him and the prosecutor describes him as 'a perjured, murdering villain and Jewish doctor worse than Judas himself'. Lopes is found guilty of treason.

The queen doesn't believe it and even after he's found guilty, she has him brought from his prison cell to treat her in March. She puts off signing the death warrant for as long as possible but Devereux and Robert Cecil persuade her that justice must be seen to be done or other would-be assassins might try their hand. Elizabeth is forced to confirm the sentence and on 7 June poor Lopes is dragged to Tyburn Hill and hanged. He cries out that he loves Queen Elizabeth as he loves Jesus Christ but the crowd boo and shout him down. He is the only royal physician to be executed in England so you will realise that nobody is safe at the Tudor court … or anywhere else in Elizabethan England.

A playwright, an atheist and a spy

We don't know the names of many spies, double agents and informants in the Elizabethan intelligence network, apart from Gifford, who assisted the unravelling of the Babington plot, and Roger Lopes because their names are secret, but we may know of another: Christopher 'Kit' Marlowe, playwright, atheist and, maybe, sometime spy. Let's ask Kit to tell us something of his life:

'Good day to you, Master Marlowe. As a famous playwright, readers would like to know more about you. What of your early life and education?'

'I was born in Canterbury in Kent in February 1564.'

'So you're only two months older than William Shakespeare.'

'That charlatan! Do you want to hear about me or not?'

'I apologise.'

'My father was a shoemaker, so we didn't have much money to spare and I was one of nine children but, as the eldest son, my parents wanted me to be educated. Fortunately, my genius was soon apparent and I won scholarships, firstly to King's School in Canterbury and then, when I was sixteen, to Corpus Christi College, Cambridge. I was a brilliant student, of course, yet the university was reluctant to award my Master of Arts degree in 1587.'

'Why was that?'

'Oh some utter nonsense about my planning to go to France to train for the Roman Catholic priesthood. As if I would. It's illegal for an Englishman to do that and besides … keep this to yourself … I'm not convinced that God even exists.'

'What! You're an atheist?'

'Shh.'

'But that's also a criminal offence.'

'I know but you see how absurd it is to believe the rumours? Mind you, I'm not saying I wasn't attending a school for priests in France from time to time while I was studying at Cambridge.'

'Tell me more.'

'Francis Walsingham recruited me as one of his intelligence gatherers. That's why I was in France. It was the Privy Council who wrote to the university, commanding them to give me my degree, declaring that I shouldn't have it withheld because of my "faithful dealing and good service" to Her Majesty, as well as "matters touching the benefit of my country". I was paid well for the information I obtained, enabling me to live far better than my pittance of a scholarship allowed.'

'But then you were in trouble in London in 1589 and didn't you spend time in Newgate Gaol?'

'More nonsense and a misunderstanding is all. My neighbours got in a fight. I tried to intervene but it ended in a fatality. We were all arrested but I was released on bail and eventually acquitted at the trial and quite rightly so.'

'And then you were arrested in the Netherlands in 1592 and hauled back to England, although the charges were immediately dropped.'

'Of course they were. I was sent there by the Privy Council to infiltrate a nest of Catholic conspirators, led by William Stanley. Among other things, they were making counterfeit English coins, hoping to undermine our trading links. But my cover was blown. My arrest was the safest means of escape.'

'And now, in May 1593, you're threatened with arrest again, this time for atheism.'

'It's Thomas Kyd's fault. He also calls himself a playwright and is insanely jealous of my far superior talent. He said of me that I am blasphemous, disorderly, holding treasonous opinions, being an irreligious reprobate, intemperate and of a cruel heart. How dare the slanderous devil! I went to see the Privy Council this morning to sort this out but there was no meeting. I've been told to present myself daily for the convenience of their lordships but … Oh, I espy a wretch who claims I owe him money. Farewell in haste…'[3]

That conversation happened on 20 May. On Wednesday 30 May, Kit Marlowe is slain in suspicious circumstances. At the inquest held on that Friday by the Coroner Queen's Household, William Danby, witnesses claim that Marlowe spent all day in an ale-house owned by Eleanor Bull in Deptford, then a Thameside village southeast of London. Kit was drinking there with three others: Ingram Frizer, Nicholas Skeres and Robert Poley. Frizer describes himself as a servant of Thomas Walsingham (Francis's second cousin) at Scadbury Manor in Kent (see page 129). Thomas is a patron and friend of Kit who spends so much time at Scadbury Manor that it's the first place the authorities looked for him to arrest him a few weeks earlier. So Kit and Frizer probably know each other quite well. The other two, Skeres and Poley, have worked as Francis Walsingham's spies in uncovering the conspirators in the Babington plot.

Christopher Marlowe, (probably), 1585.

Witnesses state that Marlowe and Frizer argued over who should pay the bill, exchanging 'divers malicious words'. Frizer was sitting at a table between the other two and Marlowe was lying behind him on a couch. Marlowe snatched Frizer's dagger and wounded him on the head. In the struggle which followed, Marlowe was stabbed above the right eye and died immediately. The jury concludes that Frizer acted in self-defence and within a month he is pardoned. Marlowe is buried in an unmarked grave in the churchyard of St Nicholas, Deptford immediately after the inquest, on 1 June 1593.

However, even today, knowledge of the incident leading to Marlowe's death remains questionable and the full story may never be known. The witnesses are the very people involved and Robert Poley is described as a rogue, a liar and 'the very genius of the Elizabethan underworld'. Nicholas Skeres is not only a spy but a known confidence-trickster who runs a money-lending racket. Why should we believe their version of events? How is it that the inquest report honours these men with the title 'gentlemen', which they most certainly are not?

There is even a hint that Kit Marlowe's death is faked. This could be arranged by the Privy Council who fear that, if he's brought to trial for atheism, he knows far too much about their involvement in clandestine activities at home and abroad. Things could become very messy for Lord Burghley and his son and successor, Robert Cecil. Better to let Master Marlowe escape abroad or assume a new identity. As Burghley says at the time, 'I find the matter as in a labyrinth: easier to enter into it than to go out.'

Top Tip

One thing is certain: DON'T TRUST ANYBODY at the Tudor court because they may well be a spy.

Chapter 9

Travel

As a traveller yourself, you'll likely be interested in continuing to visit places you've never been before. Even if you have travelled widely in the twenty-first century, anywhere you went then is going to be very different in the sixteenth. So where might you go and how will you get there?

Travel by road

Most of the roads in England aren't much better than farm tracks: pot-holed and rutted. In dry weather they turn to dust and when it rains, they become a sea of mud. Pack horses, carts and covered wagons wear deep ruts in the mud which dry or freeze into ankle-breaking and axle-snapping hazards for everyone, whatever their mode of travel. In theory, each village and parish is responsible for repairing its own roads, but until 1555 there is nobody in charge to organise the work. In that year, a law is passed requiring one villager or parishioner to serve as Surveyor of the Highway for a year.

The surveyor's task is to order the local wealthy people to supply the materials to mend the roads and to organise the poor to do the labouring, doing six days of unpaid heavy work each. The rich hate to waste their money and because it's legal for the surveyor to take stone, rubble, sand or whatever is required to mend the road from their land, you can imagine the heated arguments that may happen, especially if the landowner has a building project of his own underway and the surveyor helps himself to the materials. As for the poor, they have better things to do to make a living, so being the surveyor is the most unpopular job in town. He's often ignored completely and ends up paying for the cheapest materials and labourers to do a shoddy repair and only bothers to mend the sections of road that take most traffic. Or maybe the work doesn't get done at all.

In London and a few other major towns, like York, Norwich and Bristol, some of the streets are paved but by the time Queen Elizabeth is on the throne, a new mode of transport is causing chaos – coaches. Only the rich can afford these huge, cumbersome, well-furnished chambers on wheels. Broader and heavier than most carts, they break up the paving and block the narrower streets. Coachmen come to blows and passengers lose their tempers over who should have right of way when two coaches meet and there's no room to pass. Pedestrians had better watch out too, or get crushed against a wall.

If you travel on horseback and the weather is reasonable, it will probably take you about a week to ride from London to York. A decent horse can manage fifty miles a day at a steady pace, requiring rests and refreshment along the way, and so will you. And it's expensive. Not only will you have to pay for your own food and lodgings every night but for your horse as well. A royal messenger, though, can manage the journey in a couple of days because he picks up a fresh horse at each stage, but the man will arrive exhausted.

Travelling by road has dangers, apart from accidents due to the highway itself and broken bridges, or such natural obstacles

Did You Know?

Soon after Elizabeth's successor, James I, comes to reign in England, London makes an attempt to ease congestion and frayed tempers by introducing the first one-way streets in the lanes which run either side of Thames Street, down by the river. Yes, that particular drivers' bugbear has been around that long!

Travel

as fallen or overhanging trees and flooding. Some hazards are entirely human: highwaymen – or women. The Tudor age is one of growing population and mass unemployment and desperate people are forced into a life of crime just to survive. In the twenty-first century, highwaymen – like their sea-going equivalent, pirates – have an air of romance about them but, at the time, there is nothing romantic about thieves and ruffians assaulting travellers and taking their valuables, sometimes using that recent lethal invention, the pistol, to force coachmen or riders to stop.

One Elizabethan who turns to crime is a woman known as Moll Cut-Purse. Let's have a word with Moll.

'Good day to you Moll.'

'A good day? I think not. I've just been branded on me 'and. Look.'

'What did you do to deserve that?'

'Stole two shillin's an' eleven pence, that's all.'

'How old are you, Moll?'

'I was born just near St Paul's in 1584, so that means I'm, er, 16 or thereabouts.'

'And already branded a thief. Moll Cut-Purse isn't your real name, is it?'

'Nah. I was christened Mary Frith but I like Moll better. Only me father ever called me Mary. He was a shoemaker, daft enough t' reckon makin' shoes was a good life. Not for me, it ain't. I'm goin' t' be rich one day. Though me uncle had ideas about packin' me off on a ship t' New England, t' make a new life. He's a churchman, see. Says I'm a disgrace t' womanhood, daft ol' fool. Anyway, I wasn't goin' t' America, now was I? So I jumps overboard and swims t' land and here I am, back in London where I belongs.'

'Why does your uncle think you're a disgrace to womanhood?'

'Got eyes, ain't yer? Cos I dresses like a man, o' course, an' I cuss an' swear an' drink in taverns and pick fights like a roarin' boy and I smokes a pipe o' tobacco like Walter Raleigh hisself. An' I can ride better than any o' them. But I'm better known – as yer might guess from me nickname – as the best cut-purse in town. Nobody feels me stealin' their valuables and I'm long gone before they realise. In fact, I'm so well known fer it, if folks discover they've been robbed in the street, they comes t' me t' buy it back. [Cackles loudly, slapping her thigh.] Now ain't that a laugh? I get rich either way. Other rogues bring me stuff they've stoled to sell on too. I 'ave quite a proper business goin' on.'

'Do you intend to mend your ways, Moll?'

'Course not. Life's fun, ain't it? I might run a bawdy 'ouse, or act on a stage…'

'Women aren't allowed to go on stage.'

'Get away, yer mouldy ol' Puritan. I dresses like a man: I acts like a man. I'll go on stage, if I wants to. An' I tell yer what … I quite fancy bein' a highwayman … horse an' pistols an' a mask over me face.'

'On the stage, do you mean?'

'Nah. Fer real, holdin' up rich folks in their coaches then disappearin' into the night like a phantom … Mm. I might try that some day.'

'Don't you want to marry and have children?'

'Pooh, not me. I s'pose I might marry, if I finds it more, er, convenient, but babies – never! I likes dogs and parrots better than babies – squawkin' little brats are too much trouble. And when I die, yer knows, I'm goin' t' shock 'em all cos I'll put in me will that I wants t' be buried wearin' men's breeches … back t' front. There! Even God'll be shocked at the sight o' me. Make Him laugh, though, won't it?'

'Yes, Moll, it probably will.[1]

And Moll Cut-Purse goes on to do all those things, including being a highwayman, living until 1659 when she is, indeed, buried wearing men's clothing and with her breeches on backwards.

All at sea

Unsurprisingly, wherever feasible, going by boat on river or sea is a more comfortable alternative and less likely to shake goods to pieces and shred passengers' nerves, although bad weather and the possibilities of shipwreck and piracy mean it isn't always safer.

One famous Tudor ship which is wrecked, having barely left the harbour, is the *Mary Rose*. Henry VIII's flagship and the very latest in maritime technology, she is sunk by the French in full view of the king, in the battle of the Solent – the stretch of water separating Portsmouth from the Isle of Wight, off the south coast of England, on 19 July 1545. Of the 400 or more men on board, only thirty-five survive to tell the tale. The ship sinks so fast, anyone below decks has little chance of escape, including Sir George Carew who was created a vice-admiral and named as captain of Henry's favourite vessel only the day before.[2]

Seafaring in the sixteenth century is, literally, changing the world. Gerard Mercator (1512–94), a Flemish-born German working in the Netherlands, is famous for his vast knowledge of geography, his detailed atlases, globes and navigational maps

Did You Know?

It has always been assumed that the idea of mounting compasses on gimbals, so the instruments remain level despite the movement of the ship, was not introduced until the seventeenth century. Yet there were three examples discovered on the *Mary Rose*, the earliest in Europe.

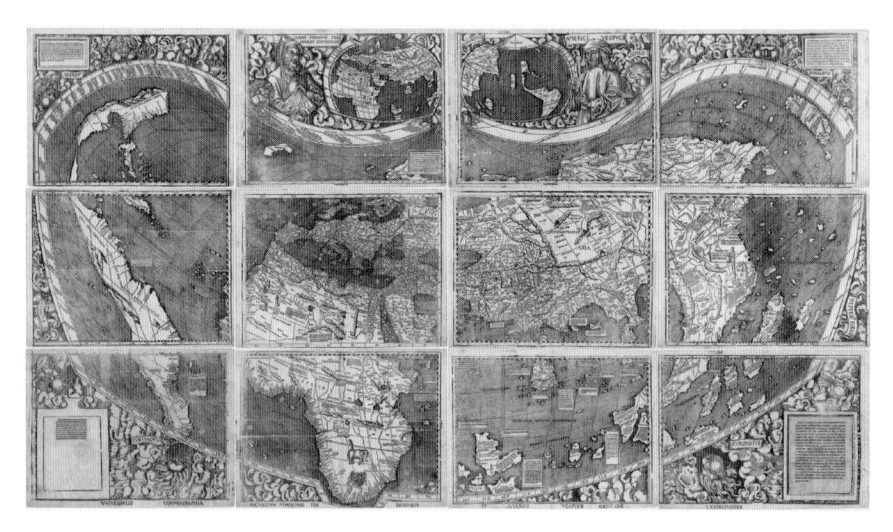

World map drawn on twelve separate sheets, showing South American coast and Caribbean islands with Florida (top) on far left.

for mariners – all produced without ever leaving home. Instead, he uses his huge library of over 1,000 books, and corresponds in six different languages with merchants, scholars and seamen who travel across the world. In 1541, he produces a marvellous globe, showing the world as it is now known, with quite a degree of detail for the eastern coast of America but the western coast remains vague, guesswork for the most part.

In 1547, the young English scholar, John Dee – later the Queen's Magician – visits Mercator. They get along well together, sharing their fascination for maps and instruments and remain fervent correspondents for decades to come, until Mercator's death. Dee spends time with Mercator during his three years of study at Louvain University and brings assorted maps, globes and astronomical instruments back to England. This isn't a one-way trade; in return Dee sends Mercator copies of the latest English texts on all sorts of subjects that might prove of interest, and most importantly any new geographical knowledge discovered as a result of English explorations of the world.

Perhaps the most significant contribution would be Sir Francis Drake's logbook and reports of his circumnavigation of the world in 1577–80. However, despite proving, once and for all, that the earth is a sphere, for political reasons, Drake says very little about his voyage that is made public. This is mainly because he has been harassing Spanish territory in the New World and waylaying their treasure-laden galleons at sea, so the less said about that, the better. Drake also explores the Pacific coast of America, perhaps as far north as Alaska, and the English have no intention of revealing their knowledge and discovery of these places to others, especially not the Spaniards who are the enemy. Eventually, Drake circumnavigates the globe. What an adventure that must be.

If you have the courage and long to explore far beyond England, perhaps you could join a ship's crew, like that of Drake's *Golden Hind*. But beware, it's a hazardous life and sometimes you don't even have a choice. In 1582, the English writer, Richard Hakluyt, hits on a solution: why not empty the gaols of England by sending the felons to America? The idea of the transportation of convicts to the colonies gradually catches on; the poor sometimes volunteer to go in the hope of making a fresh start with a more hopeful future and, for some, it works out well. For others, it ends in tragedy.

Did You Know?

In the seventeenth century, when the English begin to colonise the eastern seaboard of North America, they actually lay claim to the entire expanse of the continent, from 'sea to shining sea', as they put it. This is done on the grounds that Drake had landed in California, most likely in what becomes San Francisco Bay, on 15 June 1579, naming the land *Nova Albion,* (New England in Latin and predating New England on the eastern seaboard of North America) claiming it in the name of Queen Elizabeth and planting the English flag there.

The American dream

In 1584–85, Sir Walter Raleigh sponsors the first English colony in America on Roanoke Island, now in North Carolina but then in Virginia, named for Elizabeth as the Virgin Queen, although the locals call it Wingandacoa. Raleigh's agents – he never sets foot there in person – wanting to persuade would-be colonists, paint a rosy picture of the new country: 'The land smells sweetly as if we be in the midst of some delicate garden'; 'The soil is so fertile that a day's labour in planting will provide food for a year.' Despite the advertising, this is not a venture for anyone expecting an easy existence and stupendous profits. In fact, the colony fails and another attempt at colonisation also fails in 1587. You may wonder what makes the English believe they have the right to colonise there at all? The land must belong to someone: Spain, according to the Treaty of Tordesillas.

However, the Spaniards haven't come this far north on the East Coast of America, so haven't claimed the land. A clause in the treaty specifies that new lands are only up for grabs so long as they are 'uninhabited by any Christian prince'. Although the English aren't even mentioned in the treaty they, along with the Dutch, the French and any other European nation wanting to expand their horizons, take that phrase to mean any territory occupied by 'heathen savages', i.e. by peoples not already Christianised, is available for exploitation and colonisation. Although that phrase serves for now, it won't be long before the 'Christian princes' are fighting among themselves over all desirable lands.

One of the first English settlers to arrive in Virginia in the 1585 attempt at colonisation is John White, a London gentleman, map-maker and artist who paints watercolour images of the local peoples, the wildlife and landscape of the new land.

Let's ask Master White about his times in Virginia:

> 'Master John, you've made two attempts to set up a colony and live in the New World. Can you tell us what happened and why you are now back in England?'

John White's watercolour of a Native American of Roanoke, 1585.

'Things never quite worked out as Sir Walter Raleigh hoped. It was his idea to found the Roanoke Colony in 1585. It proved a disaster. Too many gentlemen who didn't want to get their hands dirty and too few who were willing and knew anything about growing crops. The local people grew all manner of vegetables and hunted and fished but our knowledge of how to feed ourselves through a hard winter was utterly lacking. Anyway, Roanoke soil was poor and the area unhealthy, so we abandoned the attempt. I told Master Hakluyt the place isn't fit even for him to send criminals from the gaols.'

'But Sir Walter Raleigh had made you Governor of Roanoke by then.'

'Governor of a Lost Cause, I reckon.'

'But you returned to begin again?'

'That wasn't our intension, I assure you. Full of hope, in May 1587, we planned to found a colony in Chesapeake Bay, a place we'd seen previously that looked more suitable. But our Portuguese pilot – God rot his Catholic soul – sailed us back to Roanoke, put us ashore and refused to let us back on board ship. He'd earned his name: we called him 'the Swine'. So we 113 colonists had to make the best of it, my daughter, Eleanor, and her husband, my assistant Ananias Dare, among them. Soon after we arrived, Eleanor gave birth to a child, my granddaughter, the first Christian soul ever born in North America. We named her Virginia after our new home, as we hoped. That was in August: too late to make any attempt to plant crops and our supplies wouldn't last the winter, so I returned to England for more provisions since the supply ships believed we were in Chesapeake Bay. My voyage was one disaster after another. By the time I reached England, we were at war with Spain and any ships that weren't warships were kept in port by royal command. Then there came the terror of the Spanish Armada.'

'But you did see Roanoke once more?'

'Yes. My granddaughter would have been three years old by then. My supplies came far too late. There was no sign of the colonists – not one. They'd left a message carved on a tree trunk which suggested they might have moved on to Croatoan Island. We travelled there and I searched and searched, reluctant to give up hope, but never found them. Who knows? Maybe my daughter and her family are still there, somewhere in Virginia, but…'

'I hope you find them someday, Master John.'

'I will never go to the New World again. I'm too old for such adventures but I have my paintings to remind me of that strange place with its weird flora and fauna and incomprehensible people. Who knew that God created so many wonders we had never seen before?[3]

Among the strange new crops and wonders of the Americas, Sir Walter Raleigh is credited with bringing potatoes and tobacco back to Britain and his influence at court certainly makes smoking popular there. Although the queen doesn't take up the habit, many others do. Tobacco is believed to have health-giving properties. Maybe you can persuade your Tudor friends otherwise and save us all from the problems of smoking in the centuries to come.

Exploring Europe

Of course, you don't have to go all the way to America or around the world, if you want to visit foreign places and have adventures. Europe is closer and just as lively – and dangerous.

We have already met, briefly, the Welshman, John Dee – he is a witness against Dr Roger Lopes (Chapter 8) and a correspondent with the map-maker, Mercator. Dee was born in 1527 and became a brilliant scholar at Cambridge University, where he reckoned he studied for eighteen hours a day to earn his MA. by the time he was 21. Although he doesn't get his doctorate in medicine until 1585 from the University of Prague, he seems to have given himself the title 'Dr' long before that.

Dee is an excellent mathematician and collects a huge library of thousands of manuscripts and books at a time when a dozen volumes are considered a notable collection. Also, he has no doubts about the existence of magical powers and wants to put them to good use. He first comes to the notice of royalty in 1551 when Sir William

Cecil recommends him to King Edward VI who, upon receiving two astronomical texts that Dee has written and dedicated to the young monarch, awards him a sizeable annual pension of 100 crowns.

But after Edward's death two years later, his Catholic half-sister, Queen Mary, has no use for Dee. In fact, in 1555, Mary has Dee arrested, charged with drawing up the horoscopes of the queen, her husband Philip of Spain, and Princess Elizabeth, Mary's heir, in order to foretell their futures. This is a treasonous activity: attempting to discover when a monarch will die. Dee is also accused of 'conspiring by enchantments to destroy Queen Mary'. Whether he calculated her date of death or not, it is probably fortunate that Mary dies before any serious actions are taken against him, although he is questioned closely by the Bishop of London concerning his religious beliefs. These are dangerous times and a man interrogated alongside Dee isn't so lucky and burns at the stake.

Perhaps when he casts Princess Elizabeth's horoscope, Dee foresees a long reign and better success for himself. Elizabeth's reign begins very well for Dee when Robert Dudley, the queen's favourite, summons him to court, to study the star charts and determine the most propitious date for the queen's coronation. She promises Dee an even better pension, saying 'Where my brother [Edward VI] hath given him a crown [5 shillings] I will give him a noble [6 shillings and 8 pence].' Although Dee never receives any regular payments from her, he is given the occasional handout and the title of 'Queen's Magician'.

By 1564, Dee has a large house at Mortlake in Surrey, a wife and an ever-expanding library. He earns his living as a tutor of mathematics and by writing books on mathematics and navigation. He is an expert on navigation without ever having captained a ship, but he is closely involved in the search for new sea routes to India and China via the fabled North-East passage to the north of Russia or, failing that, the North-West passage through northern Canada. With the increasing English interest in colonising North America, the question arises of Elizabeth's claims to that continent and Dee is required to draw up the documents to support England's rights to the new lands there.

He makes a thorough job of it, investigating the matter all the way back to King Arthur's day, drawing a map to show that Newfoundland and other parts of the eastern coast of America were colonised by King Arthur's people so, obviously, Elizabeth has a rightful claim to sovereignty there as a descendant of Arthur. No doubt the queen is delighted to realise her prerogative and Dee is honoured with two audiences with her, as he records in his diary.

But what of Europe? In the 1580s, Dee travels to Europe, taking his wife and family and an 'associate', Edward Kelley and his wife. As we've seen, Dee is always interested in foretelling the future, whether by horoscopes, crystal balls or consulting the spirit world; apart from astrology, he can't do these things himself, but Kelley claims he can. For years, Dee depends on Kelley 'conjuring angels' and performing all kinds of rituals according to angelic instructions. Kelley even tells Dee the angels require that they should 'swap' wives. He also insists the angels predict that their secret experiments in alchemy are on the verge of producing the Philosopher's Stone and, since they are, currently, in the lands of the Holy Roman Emperor, Rudolf II, Kelley persuades Dee to inform the emperor they will shortly be able to produce as much gold as he wants. Unsurprisingly, Rudolf is intrigued and eager so he equips a laboratory where Dee and Kelley can work. Kelley is soon, supposedly, turning lengths of wire into gold rings, claiming that one is worth £4,000, but since it's so easy to do, he gives the ring away to a lowly servant – or so he says. Rudolf sees no reason to employ Dee as well when Kelley is performing the magic alone, so Dee returns to England, leaving Kelley to fill the emperor's coffers with gold.

Spies have been reporting the goings-on at Rudolf's court to Sir William Cecil, Lord Burghley, who is keen to have Kelley perform his tricks for Queen Elizabeth's benefit. But then Kelley is arrested, accused of trying to poison the emperor. He is soon released and it seems likely that Rudolf has simply grown tired of supporting the man when no gold is ever forthcoming. Kelley fades from the records. He and Dee are fortunate that nothing worse befalls them, either in Europe or at home, what with their dabbling in the Black Arts and, literally, playing with fire.

Dee is unable to make use of Kelley's discoveries and can no longer consult the angels without him. His library has been ransacked while he was abroad and he now lives in poverty. His wife is dead and he has to sell his fine house in Mortlake. He lives on into the reign of the queen's successor, King James, a confirmed believer in witches so, wisely, the Queen's Magician keeps a low profile and dies a poor man in the spring of 1609 at the grand old age of 82. He survived the dangerous times at home and the hazards of travel in Europe.

But one who is ultimately less fortunate is Sir Philip Sidney of Penshurst Place in Kent. Philip was born in November 1554, during the reign of Mary Tudor and Philip of Spain, named after the latter who stood as his godfather. Young Philip's father, Sir Henry Sidney, is Lord Deputy of Ireland and his mother is Mary Dudley, sister of Robert Dudley, Earl of Leicester, so the Sidney family remain in royal

The Baron's Hall, Penshurst Place, Kent, birthplace of Sir Philip Sidney.

Exterior view of Penshurst Place, Kent.

favour when Elizabeth becomes queen. Despite having a Roman Catholic king as his godfather, Philip is very much a Protestant and sometimes too much so to please Elizabeth, who prefers moderation in religious matters.

Philip is well educated and attends Christ Church College, Oxford, before going off on a tour of Europe to complete his education as is becoming the fashion for young gentlemen. In August 1572, he has his first brush with danger in Paris during the St Bartholomew's Day Massacre of French Protestant Huguenots, and English Protestants would seem to be fair game as well. For ten days, Philip and his friends hole up at Quai des Bernadins, in a house owned by Sir Francis Walsingham that is used as a sort of English embassy, not daring to venture out. Philip's uncle, Robert Dudley, writes to him, ordering him to come home as soon as possible, but Philip has already escaped Paris before the letter arrives. He and his friends ride eastwards, leaving France as the killing of Protestants spreads out from the capital. They reach Heidelberg before the end of September. Here, Philip meets some of the most interesting people in Europe of different nationalities and every theological persuasion with architects, engineers, composers and writers among them. He meets Charlotte de Bourbon, the daughter of a French duke. Charlotte has lately walked out of the convent where she was the abbess in charge, thrown aside her nun's habit and will later marry the divorcee William of Orange. Philip and his friends have been suspected previously of 'lewd behaviour' but, clearly, scandalous goings-on are happening everywhere in sixteenth-century Europe; the activities of a 17-year-old Englishman are hardly remarkable.

Philip spends three years travelling around Central Europe, visiting Frankfurt, Strasberg, Geneva, Vienna, Padua in Italy, back to Vienna, then to Cracow in Poland, where he falls ill, probably suffering from exhaustion after so much travelling. But as soon as he recovers, he journeys to Prague in Bohemia and, apparently, most of his travels are done on horseback with mules carrying the baggage. Europe's inland rivers and waterways are often silted up and extortionate tolls are charged for those going anywhere by boat – unlike in England where rivers are the easiest and cheapest means of getting around. Via Saxony and Hesse, Philip finally returns home to England, having seen and experienced the worst and best of the European experience and met all manner of fascinating personalities.[4]

However, in 1577, Philip's knowledge of Europe and its peoples make him the queen's choice as ambassador to the new Holy Roman Emperor Rudolph II, and to William of Orange, known as William the Silent, who had recently wed Charlotte de Bourbon. His remit is to take the queen's condolences to both men on the deaths of their fathers but, by the way, to test out the possibilities of forming a Protestant League. Yet Philip's brand of Protestantism proves a little too enthusiastic for Elizabeth's liking and she summons him back to court.

At court, Philip writes poetry and becomes the patron of other aspiring young poets like Edmund Spenser of *Faerie Queene* fame. He's the perfect, chivalrous courtier until he falls from the queen's favour when he not only writes a long letter to her explaining why she shouldn't marry her current suitor, the French Duke of Alençon, who's far too young for her and – worse still – a Catholic, but he then challenges the Earl of Oxford – Alençon's champion at the English court – to a duel! The queen is seriously displeased and Philip has the good sense to retire from court until things cool off.

In 1583, he marries Frances, the daughter of Sir Francis Walsingham, even though his first love, Penelope Devereux, to whom he wrote his sonnets, has been married off against her wishes to Robert Rich, Earl of Warwick. It is possible that Penelope's father, Walter Devereux, Earl of Essex (father of Robert Devereux in Chapter 8) intended Philip to marry his daughter but when Walter dies, her brother forces her to wed Rich instead. Perhaps as compensation and to prove she is no longer displeased with him, the queen gives Philip a knighthood along with a bride.

But Sir Philip is finding life as a courtier and a husband too dull and feels in need of more foreign adventures. In 1585, despite the queen having forbidden him, he tries to sneak on board one of Francis Drake's ships bound for Cadiz, hoping to take part in the expedition Drake later describes as 'the singeing of the King of Spain's beard'. Elizabeth summons him back to court but, realising his restlessness, she gives him a new position, making him Governor of Flushing in the Netherlands where England is supporting the Dutch in their revolution against their hated Spanish overlords.

Now 31, Philip is still a rash young man, complaining that his uncle, Robert Dudley – who is in command in the Netherlands – is being too cautious. Unsurprisingly, Philip is not only eager to fight but takes one risk too many. At the 'battle' of Zutphen (more of a skirmish) on 22 September 1586, seeing his men wearing less armour than he is, Philip throws off some of his personal protection – so the story goes – including his thigh guards. A musket shot shatters his thigh bone: a wound Tudor medicine can do nothing to mend. As he lays wounded in the field, it's said that the hero gives his water bottle to an injured soldier whose need is greater than his own. Philip dies slowly of gangrene but continues composing poetry on his deathbed. The Elizabethan court and all England mourn the loss of the perfect, chivalrous courtier. His body is brought home and buried in St Paul's Cathedral.

So a warning note here: however adventurous you are, heroism is to be avoided, if you hope to survive in Tudor times.

Sir Philip Sidney, 1554–86, after Antonis Mor.

Chapter 10

Leisure Time

In Tudor England, a whole new facet of life is evolving, at least for those who can afford it – leisure. And leisure requires a number of pastimes to fill it, so there have to be people to arrange and provide these pastimes, which leads to a variety of jobs that hardly existed before. If you have the imagination, becoming a poet like Sir Philip Sidney is an option as literacy spreads among the middle and upper classes but to become popular with those who cannot read, being a playwright is the up and coming thing. Everyone, from shoemakers' sons from Canterbury and glovers' sons from Stratford-upon-Avon to London school teachers, tries their hand at writing scripts for comedies, tragedies, romances and histories to amuse the public flocking to the theatres around the capital or going on the road, to draw the crowds out in the sticks.

Writing for money

Literate Tudors with time to spare may amuse themselves by writing for pleasure. It's thought that Thomas More penned his scathing indictment of Richard III with no intention of publishing it – that was

> **Top Tip**
>
> Even if you're not much of a playwright yourself, it's common to co-write plays so you can still get your name up there on the advertising playbills, if not 'top of the bill' then as a co-author. This should be easy if you already know a Shakespeare play or two as yet unwritten. You can beat the Bard to it. After all, he is always stealing other writers' material.

done after his death by his son-in-law – but just for his own interest. The Elizabethans take to composing sonnets and love poetry, often dedicated to an unnamed beloved, but it is becoming possible to earn a reasonable income with your pen, so let's look at some of the genres you could try.

'Interludes' are an early Tudor invention: comic, amusing and often bawdy. These one-act farces have little in the way of plot, more like modern comedy sketches. John Heywood writes a number of them, including *John-John, Tib and Sir John* in a domestic love triangle with plenty of silly action, mistaken kisses and erroneous assumptions. But, gradually, audiences want more depth of character and proper plots, although 'interludes' don't entirely disappear. As brief musical or comedy sketches, they are performed at the front of the stage as cover for scenery or costume changes between acts in longer plays.

One of these longer plays is the five-act comedy, *Ralph Roister Doister*, written by a London schoolmaster, Nicholas Udell, between 1550 and 1553. Previously, along with the king's antiquary, John Leland, he had written some of the scripts in verse for the pageants performed for Anne Boleyn on the eve of her coronation. But let's ask Master Udell to tell us about his new play:

> 'Good day, Master Udell. Would you tell us about the plot in your comedy play?'
>
> 'Of course, although the telling is never as good as the seeing. You should attend the performance this afternoon but I'll tell you the main plot points. The hero, Ralph, is a boastful fellow who falls in love repeatedly and expects every woman to return the favour, swearing he will die if they don't. His servant, Matthew Merrygreek, has seen it all before when Ralph declares he must win Dame Constance's heart or perish in the attempt, despite Constance being promised in marriage to the absent Gawyn Goodluck. Ralph has Merrygreek take a love letter to Constance and the crux of the plot is Merrygreek's

reading of the letter aloud to the lady. He reads the words as written but with pauses and mistaken emphasis completely reversing the meaning. For example:

*Sweet mistress, whereas I love you nothing at all,
Regarding your substance and riches chief of all…*

This is how Merrygreek reads it. The lady is insulted, not surprisingly, yet the letter is intended to read:

*Sweet mistress, whereas I love you – nothing at all
Regarding your substance and riches…*

You see my clever rearrangement of the punctuation? Merrygreek gets told off and says he will read it to her again, properly. Ralph puts on his best armour and they go together to win the lady but Constance declares she would rather wed a beggar than marry Ralph. Ralph threatens the lady and returns to do battle. Having forgotten his helmet, Merrygreek gives him a bucket to wear on his head. Unable to see, Ralph doesn't realise it's Merrygreek who is hitting him, not Constance. The lady's fiancé, Gawyn Goodluck, returns home and wants everyone to be friends and invites Ralph and Merrygreek to dine against the lady's inclination, though she bows to her lord's wishes. The play ends with a choir singing and a toast to Her Majesty.'

'It sounds very funny, Master Udell. It reminds me of Laurel and Hardy.'

'Who? Are they play-makers too? It appears everyone is an aspiring thespian these days. Don't forget to join the queue early, if you want a good vantage point for the play at three o'clock this afternoon. It'll cost you a penny to stand with the groundlings in the pit. Let's pray it doesn't rain.'[1]

At the time of writing, the queen to whom the toast is drunk is Mary Tudor and there are a few references to the *Paternoster* and the Mass; nods to the Roman Church. Could that be why this merry play is not well known in the twenty-first century? *Ralph Roister Doister* sounds far more fun for youngsters to study at school than dreary *Hamlet*.

If you think you have enough talent and don't mind hard work, you can make a living as an actor, though there is always the risk that a serious outbreak of plague will close the theatres for months at a stretch, so it would be wise to save some of your earnings during the good times to see you through the bad. Going to watch a play is such a popular pastime with rich and poor alike, that during the outbreaks of the plague in 1593, 1603 and 1608 the theatres are forcibly closed, to prevent the gathering together of crowds which help spread disease.

As for your places of work, these can vary enormously, from impromptu performances in the street or at a fair to more permanent venues. The courtyards of certain inns and taverns in London are the bases for troupes of players with guaranteed audiences, and the innkeeper makes a profit on the extra food and drink sold as well as a proportion of the takings on the door. Purpose-built theatres are a logical next step. They can hold much larger audiences and have permanent stages, storage facilities, changing rooms and the opportunity for more elaborate 'extras', such as mirrors for special effects, numerous trapdoors and interchangeable backdrops.

Most theatres are open to the sky to allow the maximum light to illuminate the stage. Of course, that means the weather can close a production at any time, a washout for both actors and audiences. The earliest London theatre with a roof is *Paul's* but it's simply the converted choir school at St Paul's Cathedral, so not ideal. *The Theatre,* built by James Burbage – father of the actor Richard Burbage – at Shoreditch, just outside London's walls, and its successor, *The Curtain,* on the same site, are both unroofed.

The insalubrious area of Bankside in Southwark on the south bank of the Thames, opposite the city, becomes the 'theatre land' of the Elizabethan era. Here *The Rose, The Swan* and *The Globe* –

> **Top Tip**
>
> There are no toilet facilities and you have to leave the theatre to relieve yourself outside.

all unroofed venues – vie for audiences, raising their flags aloft at 3 o'clock each afternoon when a performance is about to begin. Play bills are posted up beforehand, advertising the play to be staged. But be aware, audiences do not sit quietly. Conversations continue if the action is dull and disapproval is shown by booing, cat-calls and throwing things at the offending actors.

The common folk – the 'groundlings' – pay a penny to stand in the 'pit' of *The Globe* theatre. The gentry pay extra to sit in the galleries and hire cushions for comfort. The rich may watch the play from a chair set on the side of the stage itself, so they have an uninterrupted view. Anyone can attend plays, but well-to-do women often wear masks to disguise their identity.

However, during Elizabeth's reign, certain subjects, even secular ones, may be censored by the Lord Chamberlain. In fact, by William Shakespeare's time, every play must have official approval before it can be performed publicly. This means that some otherwise innocuous dramas are banned or require pruning of sensitive material. References to religion, politics or even the queen's age aren't permitted and the theatre is policed to see there is no infringement of the censorship laws. This situation leads to the development of a kind of underground theatre with short dramas on illegal themes requiring a minimum of props. The idea is that the play ends and everything is packed away before the authorities arrive to stop it and arrest players and patrons alike, but it's a risky business. Best stick to plays about historical arch-villains, like the one Shakespeare wrote between 1592–94 on the subject of the king whom the queen's grandfather, Henry VII, defeated in battle a century ago.

If, like me, you love a good novel, perhaps you can make a living as a novelist. Surprisingly, the first known novel in English

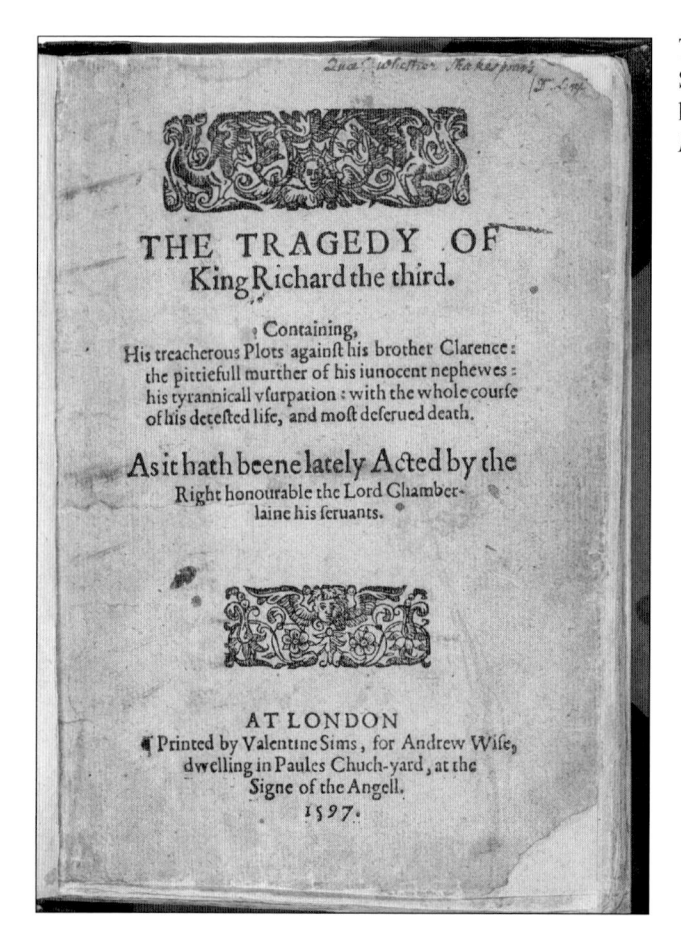

The title page of Shakespeare's historical tragedy *Richard III*, 1597.

is written in 1553, when Edward VI is king. *Beware the Cat!*[2] is penned by William Baldwin, a printer's assistant and a poet who has already had his sonnets published in 1547, the first known of that poetic form in English. King Edward is an enthusiastic Protestant, as is William, and his innovative book contains quite a bit of anti-Catholic satire. So, when the king dies in the summer of 1553 and his pro-Catholic sister Mary becomes queen, the book's publication is put on hold. Editions date from 1561, 1570 and 1584. In the twenty-first century, *Beware the Cat!* would probably be shelved under the 'Fantasy-Horror' category. From the title, you may guess that William's book, written in three parts, is not one for cat-lovers.

The novel begins at the royal court of Edward VI during the Christmas festivities of 1552. Baldwin was there in real life, working as an actor for George Ferrers, the Master of the King's Pastimes. The fiction unrolls as Baldwin tells how he and Ferrers are talking with Master Willot – Ferrers' astronomer – and Master Gregory Streamer about whether or not animals are able to think and reason. Streamer believes they can and sets out to convince the others. The rest of the book consists of his story, attempting to persuade Baldwin, Ferrers and Willot that animals cannot only reason but have discussions in their own languages.

Baldwin's use of so many characters, each of them contributing to the narrative, is beautifully done and unusual for Tudor storytelling. The dialogue is surprisingly 'modern' once the reader is used to the print type where 'u' and 'v' are transposed and 'f' is easily mistaken

The first page of a later edition of William Baldwin's novel *Beware the Cat!* originally written in 1553. This 1570 edition has a woodcut illustration of the cat, a rat (?) and a hedgehog, as well as the dedication to the Elizabethan courtier John Yong.

for the long 's'. His description of Tudor London is quite vivid. As a satire, Baldwin criticises the Catholic religious practices which aren't permitted during Edward's reign. He makes fun of the superstitious Catholic huntsmen who give Streamer the animal remains for his potion but shrink away when he mentions the 'urchin' or hedgehog, much as actors today hate any mention of 'the Scottish play'. Baldwin also mocks the scholar and the astronomer who think they know it all, as well as those foolish Catholics who believe in witches and ridiculous magic potions.

William Baldwin may not be listed with Defoe, Austen and Dickens as great writers of their day, but as England's first-ever attempt at novel writing, *Beware of the Cat!* is a fine piece of narrative fiction. Perhaps you may write a work of fiction even earlier, in the reign of Henry VIII and beat Baldwin to being the first English novelist.

Playing games

If you're going to fit in with the people around you, it will help if you have some idea of the games they enjoy and how to play them but, I warn you, the Tudors are terrible gamblers, although perhaps that's not so surprising when life itself is such a risky business. Card games, dice games, skittles and tennis matches – or even two flies crawling on a window are worth a wager. In January 1569, England holds its first ever National Lottery and with a jackpot of £5,000, it's certainly worth winning, if you can afford a ticket at 10 shillings each. If you can't, all is not lost because you and your friends can buy a ticket between you and share the prize. And yes: every ticket is a winner! Sales are in aid of updating the defences of the realm because, as ever, the Exchequer is a bit short of cash but, surprisingly, the gambling Tudors aren't that keen on the lottery and only one tenth of the 400,000 tickets are sold. Tickets go on sale outside St Paul's Cathedral on 11 January, if you wish to buy one, although the draw doesn't take place until May.

Leisure Time

Each ticket is just a piece of paper on which you write your name and a 'unique device' such as a line of prayer or poetry. One ticket that survives reads: 'God send a good lot for my children and me, which [I] have had 20 by one wife truly.' I hope his poor wife gets a share of the prize which can be silver plate, tapestries or that fabulous jackpot. Tickets are drawn from an urn by a blindfolded child and another paper taken from a different pot has the prize written on it. The unique device is read out, so the winner remains anonymous, and the appropriate prize awarded later. But the lottery isn't reckoned a success and this method of raising funds ends in 1571, replaced by a tax increase to pay for repairs to coastal forts and batteries. I don't suppose that is popular either.[3]

But for common everyday games, King Henry VII has 'houses for the playing of chess, tables (backgammon), dice, cards and billiards in the gardens' at Richmond Palace, so we know the Tudor royal family enjoys playing games, many of which you may find rather familiar. Since the king's pleasures are usually copied by everyone else, as far as financial circumstance and leisure time allow, it's likely that, on a dark winter evening, the poorest Tudor subject gets out the dice or a board game to play until bedtime.

The royals are very keen on gambling on the fall of the dice with fortunes won or lost on a single roll. Henry VIII plays often, as his wardrobe accounts reveal (his personal money box). Regularly noted are sums set aside especially for dice games: at Christmas 1529, £45 is reserved specifically for dicing with the Duke of Norfolk among others. The sergeant of the wine cellar is to receive £22 10s because of the king's losses at dice, although it isn't clear whether Henry lost to the sergeant himself or whether the servant was to pay courtiers who had won, saving the king's embarrassment in settling his debts in person. In just three years, from 1529 to 1532, Henry gambles away a staggering £3,243 5s 10d on dice, card games and other sporting events. The nobles are as keen to gamble on dice among themselves. At a time when a country gentleman lives well on £20 a year, the profligate Duke of Buckingham lost over £76 to the Duke of Suffolk and others in one evening.

But the Tudor authorities disapprove when lesser folk play similar games and the government tries to license ale-houses, taverns and inns to prevent gaming of any kind. The ordinary folk should be practising with the longbow in their spare time, ready to defend England, not enjoying themselves in idle recreation. In 1542, an act is passed making it illegal for labourers, craftsmen, small farmers (husbandmen), servants, fishermen or watermen to play dice, bowls, skittles, quoits, football or tennis, except at Christmas – but court records note so many fines being paid for gaming and gambling, it's obvious the authorities' efforts are unsuccessful. Another problem for dice players is the possibility of someone using sleight of hand and weighted dice to cheat, as in this case from 1556:

> Edward Wylgres, fishemonger, enticed Thomas Pratt, gentleman, into playing unlawful and prohibited games, Wylgres having with him in his left hand false dice that at every fall of the dice came forth at his pleasure; and that by secretly removing the true dice and play with these false dice, Edward Wylgres despoiled and defrauded Thomas Pratt of four shillings and four pence.

One popular strategy game you may recognise is Three-Men's-Morris which is like Noughts-and-Crosses or Tic-Tac-Toe. There is also a more complex version known as Nine-Men's-Morris, using a square board with eight positions around the edge and one in the centre. The players take turns to put a piece or 'man' on the board, aiming to get three in a row – a 'mill'. If a mill is achieved, the player takes one of his opponent's men off the board. The game ends when one player has only two men remaining so can't make a 'mill'. There is a Tudor board game not unlike Snakes-and-Ladders called Goose. Unsurprisingly, the Tudor version involves gambling. Before the game begins, each player puts an agreed stake in the pot. If one player lands on an occupied square anywhere on the board, the two players change places and both add an agreed 'fine' to the pot. Landing on any hazard square also requires a fine paid into the pot. The winner received the entire pot.

Perhaps the most popular and intricate dice game is Hazard. An early seventeenth-century 'how-to' book, *The Complete Gamester*, gives full instructions (below), if you need to know them, but if you can work them out, please tell us.

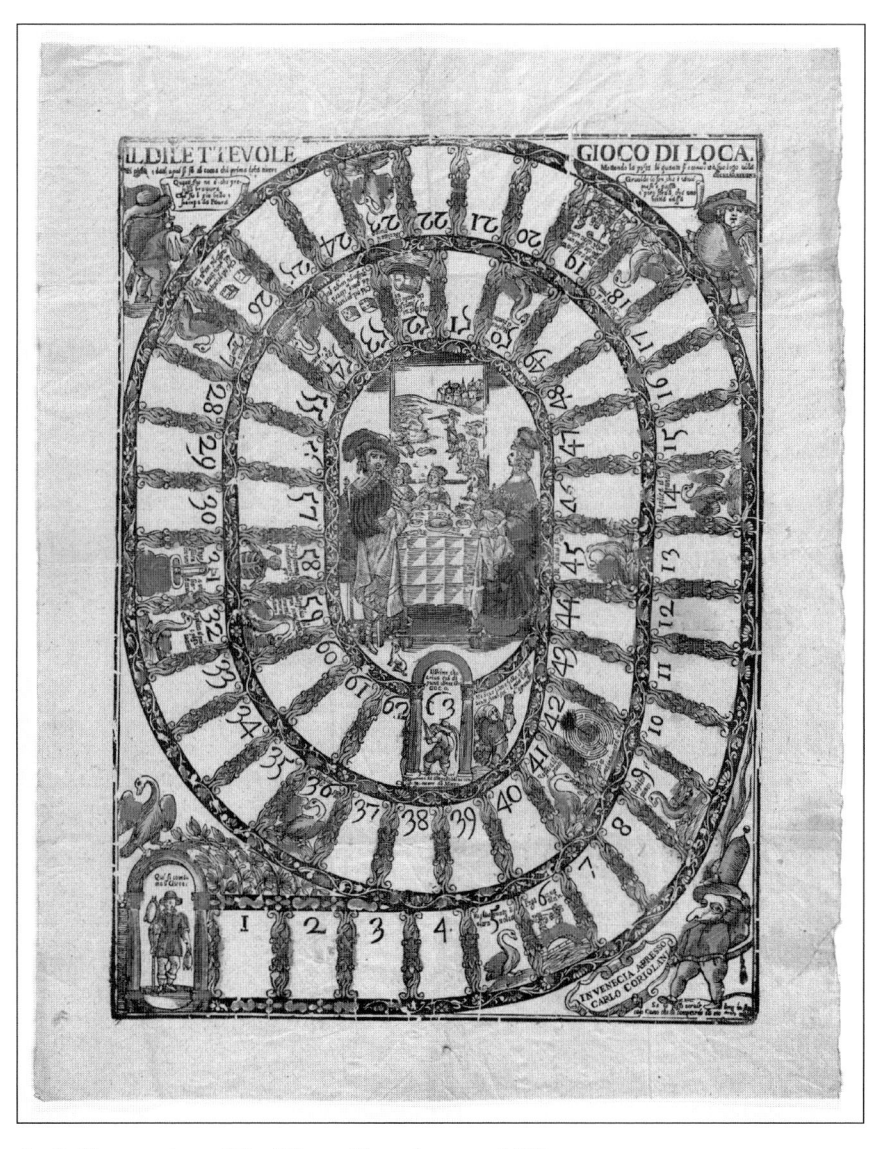

An Italian version of the 'Goose' board-game, 1589.

> **FACTS** 🔊
>
> One die is rolled and the highest begins play. The first player rolls two dice. The object is to fall within the main, any number between 5 and 9. Once the main is rolled the player continues to roll and depending upon the total of the pips he will either win, lose or continue rolling.
>
> If the player rolls a two or three, they lose (rolling a two or three after rolling the main is always a loss). Rolling a two is called an ames-ace.
>
> Depending on what number is rolled in the main, differing secondary rolls may result in a win…
>
> - If the number rolled was a five or a nine, the player need only roll within the main to win. A win is called a nick. If he rolls an eleven or a twelve they lose.
> - If the main is six or eight, the player must roll the main or a twelve to win. If they roll an eleven they lose.
> - If the main was a seven, the player must roll the main or an eleven to win. If they roll a twelve they lose.
>
> Any roll outside the main on the first roll is called a mark. The player must then continue to roll and hit the mark to win. If they roll in the main they lose. If the player wins they continue to roll. If they lose, play goes to the next player.[4]

Playing cards are originally imported into England from France around 1500. The cards are longer and narrower and the backs are blank, not patterned, as with modern packs. Despite their French heritage, there is an English tradition that the Queen of Hearts is supposed to be based on an image of Elizabeth of York, wife of Henry VII.

Tudor card games have some strange names, such as Mumchance, Click-Clack and Gleek, but Henry VIII's favourite is Primero, the forerunner of Poker. Henry never has much luck as a player since this was the game that led to his huge losses, as mentioned above.

'Four Gentlemen of High Rank playing Primero.' In this painting, the grey-bearded man, second from the right, is said to be Lord Burghley, although he once claimed he was too busy dealing with affairs of state for Queen Elizabeth to have time to waste on so frivolous a matter as playing cards.

It's played with a deck of only forty cards, leaving aside the eights, nines and tens.

Another card game with the unusual name of 'Pope Joan' is all the rage at the English court in the late 1520s. It came from France, where it was known as 'nain jaune' or 'yellow dwarf', which is how the French refer to the 9 of diamonds.[5] Pope Joan is a game for three to six players, using a pack with the eight of diamonds removed. It's said the game became symbolic of the quarrel between Henry VIII and Katharine of Aragon over the annulment of their marriage because the cards and combinations of them are named Ace, King, Queen, Jack/Knave, Pope (the 9 of diamonds), Game, Matrimony and Intrigue. There's a story that Katherine of Aragon was playing the game with her lady-in-waiting and future rival, Anne Boleyn, and seeing Anne winning the hand, said: 'Lady Anne, you have the good fortune to always stop at a king. But you are not like the others, you will have all, or none.' In this case, the stakes couldn't have been higher for both ladies.

A 'Pope Joan' gaming board.

To begin, the board is set up or 'dressed'. It has eight compartments named Pope Joan, Matrimony, Intrigue, Ace, King, Queen, Jack or Knave and Game. Each player contributes a stake: two counters or coins are put into each of the divisions Matrimony and Intrigue, one each into the other divisions and any remaining counters or coins all go into the 9 of diamonds or Pope Joan division. The fifty-one cards [the whole pack minus the 8 of diamonds] are then dealt out to the players, plus an extra hand that won't be played. The unknown cards in this hand act as 'stops' because they prevent the completion of a suit, e.g. if the 6 of clubs is in this extra hand, this will prevent the playing of the 7 of clubs. Cards are dealt so every player has the same

> **Did You Know?**
>
> The game of Pope Joan was so frequently played in Scotland, with such huge sums of money being lost, that the 9 of diamonds is known there as the Curse of Scotland.

number of cards and any remaining are added to the 'stops' hand, except for the final card which is turned over to indicate the suit of trumps.

The Ace is the lowest card; the King the highest. The player to the dealer's left plays his lowest card in a suit and names it, following with the subsequent cards of the same suit, if he has them. If he doesn't have the next card, then the player who does have it plays it, until a 'stop' is reached, i.e. a card of which the next highest in the suit lies in the extra hand not being used. All Kings are stops, as is the 7 of diamonds and every card that precedes one hidden in the extra hand or below a card that has already been played. After a stop, the player of that last card leads again with the lowest card he has.

If a player opens a round with the Ace of trumps, he takes the 'pot' from that compartment. If a round follows through to a court card of the suit of trumps (K, Q or J), then the player takes the 'pot' in the appropriate compartment. If the same player lays the Jack and Queen of trumps, he claims the Intrigue 'pot'; laying the Queen and King of trumps wins the Matrimony 'pot', and laying all three trump court cards wins both, plus the King 'pot'. If a player opens a round with his lowest card being the 9 of diamonds, he wins the Pope Joan 'pot'. In some cases, if agreed beforehand, playing the Pope Joan card may end the game. Otherwise, the first player to lay all his cards down wins the Game 'pot' and receives penalty counters or coins from each player, one for every card left in their hand, except from the player who may hold the Pope Joan card but hasn't played it. He's excused the penalty. Unclaimed stakes are left in the compartments and added to the 'pots' for the next game.

Football – England's not-so-beautiful game

If sitting around a card table isn't your thing and you want something more energetic then, as in the twenty-first century, you can play football. Quite when the game was invented we don't know, but in 1314 a law was passed banning the game in London. Despite the ban being renewed by subsequent kings, including Henry VII and Henry VIII, it's clear from the records that no one can stop this popular game. William Porlond, the clerk of the Brewers' Company of London, noted in his memorandum book that the Brewers' Hall was regularly hired for use by other City Livery Companies, Guilds and various groups. One entry notes that 'ye ffootballpleyers' hired the Hall twice in 1422–23, the earliest evidence for any kind of 'football club'.[6]

However, Tudor football is a very different game to the one you would recognise. The goals – usually the porches of two neighbouring parish churches – may be miles apart, the number of players is unlimited and the pig's-bladder ball can be picked up and thrown or kicked in an attempt to score a goal. Wrestling, punching, head-butting and hair-pulling are all allowed and injuries to players expected. Fatalities are not unknown, as Coroners' Rolls record, so be aware before you decide to join in. There are no time constraints except darkness, and a game may go on all day. The teams are often made up of men from rival villages or parishes, or married men versus apprentices, or one guild against another. Despite its rowdiness, women's matches are popular: maidens versus wives, and skirts are ideal for hiding the ball from your opponents.

In 1514, Alexander Barclay, a monk from Ely in Cambridgeshire, described a game of ball which, although it includes reference to both hands and feet, he says is called 'Foote-ball':

> They get the bladder and blowe it great and thin, with many beanes and peason put within, It ratleth, shineth and soundeth clere and fayre, While it is throwen and caste up in the eyre, Eche one contendeth and hath a great

delite, with foote and hande the bladder for to smite, if it fall to the ground they lifte it up again… Overcometh the winter with driving the foote-ball.

In *c.*1520, Richard Mulcaster, who is a teacher and headmaster at a number of English schools, is enthusiastic about football and seems to have attempted to restructure the violent game, introducing elements you will recognise. His writings refer to 'sides' and 'parties' (teams), 'a judge over the parties' (a referee), 'standings' (positions) and even a 'trayning maister (a coach). Mulcaster also suggests:

> Some smaller number [of players] with such overlooking [rules applied], sorted into sides and standings, not meeting with their bodies so boisterously to trie their strength: nor shouldring or shuffing one an other so barbarously … may use footeball for as much good to the body, by the chiefe use of the legges.

Despite kings forbidding the common folk from playing football because it interferes with their compulsory Sunday archery practice, the law doesn't apply to them or the nobility. In fact, Henry VIII's Great Wardrobe accounts note that in 1526 the king's footwear includes: 'Shoes … one leather pair for football.' The king's boots cost four shillings (nearly £100 today) and were made by his personal shoemaker, Cornelius Johnson, in 1525. They are included in the inventory made of the king's clothes when he died in 1547.

By 1572, the Bishop of Rochester is so against the violent sport he demands that the 'evil game' is outlawed for good, for rich and poor alike. As before, nobody takes any notice.

Mary, Queen of Scots is a fan because, according to Sir Francis Knollys, in 1568, at Carlisle Castle in Cumbria, the queen watched as '20 of her retinue played at football before her for 2 hours, very strongly, nimbly and skilfully'. Scotland can also lay claim to the oldest surviving football which was found hidden behind panelling

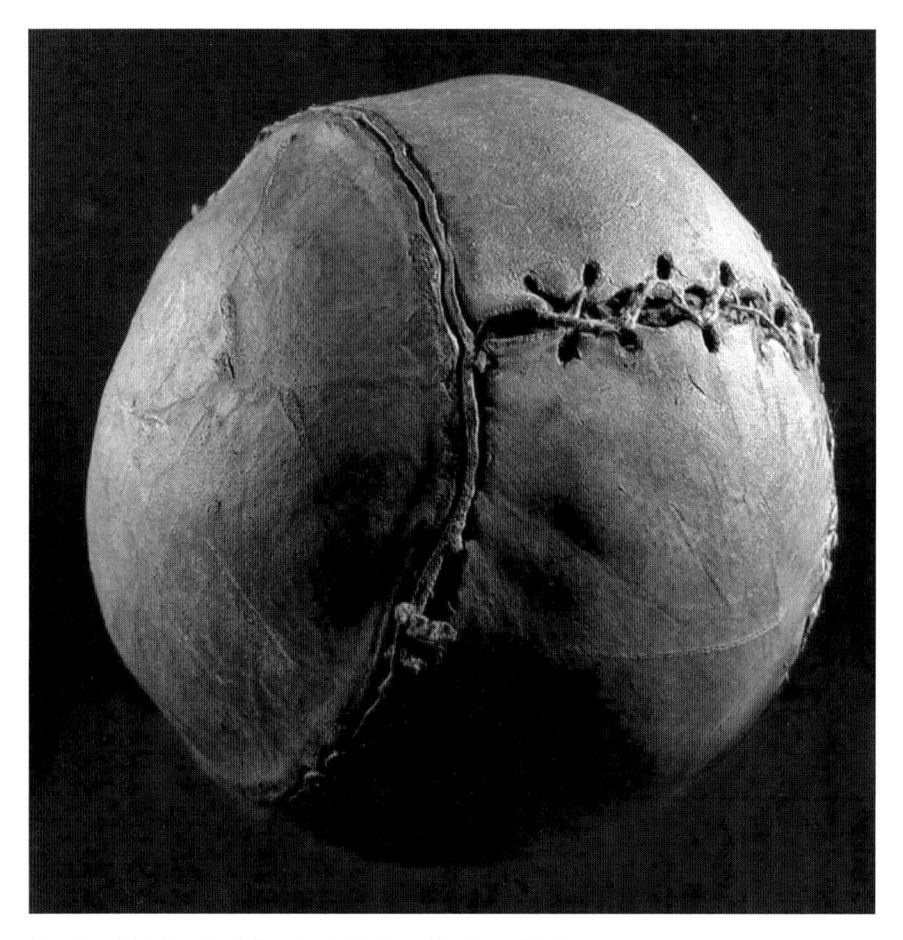

The Scottish football found at Stirling Castle, c.1540.

in The Queen's Chamber of Stirling Castle in 1981.[7] The ball dates to *c.*1540 and is made from a pig's bladder covered in leather and is approximately 6 inches (150mm) in diameter, so rather smaller than a twenty-first century football.

Music

Every Tudor gentleman and lady is expected to be able to play at least one instrument, sight-read music and sing – life will be difficult if you're tone deaf. Henry VIII plays wind, string and keyboard

Leisure Time

Elizabeth I playing the lute in miniature painted by Nicholas Hilliard.

instruments, employs lute and viol players, trumpeters and singers and ensures all his children are taught to play various instruments. The Tudor court is full of music. Elizabeth is an accomplished player on the virginals – a keyboard instrument not unlike a harpsichord – although it's said that her cousin Mary, Queen of Scots, is even more skilled, which greatly annoys Elizabeth. She tells the French ambassador that in her youth, she 'danced very well, composed balletts [*sic*] and music and played and danced them myself'.

So what kinds of music are enjoyed in the sixteenth century? Carols aren't Christmas songs but those with a repeated refrain that everyone can quickly learn and join in. They're often bawdy, lively and meant be danced to. *Blow thy horn, hunter* by William Cornysh (c.1465–1523), is all about a lusty young man chasing after a pretty maid. More refined is *The Silver Swan*, a choral work by Orlando Gibbons (1583–1625) which reflects the earlier, pre-Protestant religious music with its parts for different voices. Madrigals are a popular musical form imported from Italy, enjoyed by Elizabethans not only at court but as entertainment in less affluent homes. Again, they're written for a number of voices and usually sung unaccompanied.

In the Tudor period, music and song books are often still written by hand because early type-faces don't include notation, although pages ruled up with blank staves can be bought ready printed. Thomas Morley's *A Plain and Easy Introduction to Practical Music* is one of the first books printed with full musical scores, published in 1598 and, in the following year, he is granted a monopoly on printed music books. His *Third and Last Book of Songs,* published in 1603, after his death, brings the vibrant era of Tudor secular music and the exciting period of the dynasty to a close.

Conclusion

This concludes my handbook of helpful hints to assist you to blend in with the Tudors and Elizabethans as you explore that perilous era. Now you know how to dress and behave, eat with good manners and get along with your fellows. You also have the basics for understanding the language. If you follow my guidance, with any luck, you won't attract too much notice as you experience these exciting but dangerous times and tread the same fatal path as those unfortunates who came to a grisly end for upsetting the monarch and the authorities. Hopefully, you will be able to return to the twenty-first century to tell us of your incredible adventures in history, having 'kept your head when all about you were losing theirs.'

Don't forget to keep this useful little guide beside you at all times, in case things get tricky. It may save your life.

Bon voyage and good luck!

Notes

Chapter 1: Introduction

1. Fictionalised interview adapted from the author's *Richard III – A Man of Controversy,* (self-published booklet for students, updated 2015).

Chapter 2: Social Structure

1. Fictionalised interview adapted from Thomas Harman's pamphlet *A Caveat or Warning for Common Cursetors* (1567), British Library [https://www.bl.uk/collection-items/a-caveat-for-common-cursetors-1567#]
2. My thanks go to my friend Sandi Lowring, a National Trust volunteer at Ightham Mote, for information on Sir Richard Clement and his building projects at the Mote.
3. David Sinclair, *The Pound – A Biography* (Century, London, 2000), p.143.
4. Fictionalised interview adapted from John Guy's, *Gresham's Law – The Life and World of Queen Elizabeth I's Banker,* (Profile Books Ltd, 2019).
5. Stephen Porter, *Everyday Life in Tudor London,* (Amberley Publishing, Glos, 2016), p.213.

Chapter 3: Education and Employment Opportunities

1. The will of Sir Giles, Lord Daubeney, Chamberlain to Henry VII, PROB 11/16/405, 17 July 1509 (TNA), transcribed by the author.

2. Thomas Digges never mentions using such a piece of equipment himself but in the preface to his earlier book, *Pantometria* (1571), he mentions his father, Leonard, having invented and using the 'proportional glasses'.
3. This idea had been thought about by medieval philosophers long ago. They stated that God, being omniscient, could create as many other worlds as He wished but, mankind being His special creation, He had chosen to make only one Earth.
4. Fictionalised interview adapted from the author's article for *Tudor Life Magazine*: 'Tudor Science 2, The Tudor Universe', (2018).
5. Shakespeare mentions Lily's Latin Grammar in *Titus Andronicus, Henry IV, Part 1, The Merry Wives of Windsor* and *Much Ado about Nothing*.
6. Woodward, Marcus (ed), *Gerard's Herbal,* (Senate, Studio Editions Ltd, 1994), p.222.

Chapter 4: Religion – A Tudor Minefield

1. Fictionalised interview adapted from Richard Marius, *Thomas More* (Weidenfeld, London, 1993).
2. *English Heritage Members Magazine*, Oct 2021, p.37.
3. Fictionalised interview adapted from the author's article for *Tudor Life Magazine*: 'Thomas Norton, the 'Rackmaster' – unexpected revelations of research', (2021).

Chapter 5: Food and Health

1. From the anonymous *Boke of Kervynge,* 1500.
2. *The Boke of Nurture* (Sloane MS.2027, British Library)
3. Fictionalised interview adapted from Hilary Spurling, *Elinor Fettiplace's Receipt Book – Elizabethan Country House Cooking,* (Viking Salamander, 1986).

4. Boatwright, Habberjam & Hammond (eds), *The Logge Register of PCC Wills 1479–86* (Richard III Society, 2008), vol II, pp.39-45.
5. Also from *Elinor Fettiplace's Receipt Book,* p.187.

Chapter 6: The Problems of Fashion

1. From https://www.theanneboleynfiles.com/resources/q-a/did-anne-boleyn-wear-a-farthingale/. The additional Q&A in this article of March 2013 contains a note from Baroness von Reis, saying:

   > They [Tudor women] also wore drawers with 1 tie on the side this was optional, and men wore drawers as well, or if you want to call them knickers. The reason they tied on one side is so that you would not loose [sic] them down the lou or privey [sic], what ever you call it the camode [sic], toilet.

   (I do not know where the information originated since the baroness gives no reference – the spelling is not the best but it is interesting.)

2. Adam Hart-Davis, *What the Tudors & Stuarts Did for Us* (Boxtree, 2002), p.123.
3. *Sandwich – Ancient Town & Cinque Port, Official Guide,* (Sandwich Town Council, 2001), p.10.

Chapter 7: Home and Family

1. Fictionalised interview adapted from the Sutton House Guide Book (National Trust, 2013). When Henry VIII drew up his will after Christmas 1546, he left Ralph a bequest of £200 and appointed him to the Regency Council that would rule England while Edward VI was under age. Ralph continued his diplomatic career under Edward and held numerous offices, including Master of the Great Wardrobe which included responsibility for the Crown

Jewels. He also served Elizabeth I and one of his last duties was to sit in judgement at the trial of Mary, Queen of Scots in 1586.
2. The fine staircase at Sutton House was put in by a later owner in the seventeenth century.
3. Alison Weir, *The Six Wives of Henry VIII* (Vintage Books Ltd. Paperback version, 2007) p.460.
4. Silk sponge tampons are available on the internet, if you want to try using them before you travel back in time.
5. Jane Malcolm-Davis & Ninya Mikhaila, *The Tudor Tailor: Reconstructing Sixteenth-Century Dress* (Batsford, 2006), p.24.
6. https://www.elizabethan-era.org.uk/suitors-of-queen-elizabeth-i.htm
7. Fictionalised interview adapted from Suzannah Lipscomb, *A Visitor's Companion to Tudor England* (Ebury Press, 2012) pp. 179–82.

Chapter 8: Surviving at the Royal Court

1. My thanks go to Sandi Lowing, a friend and National Trust volunteer at Ightham Mote in Kent, for information on Richard Clement and his house, particularly for the anecdote about the 'Biblefold' panelling.
2. Alden Gregory, Assistant Curator of Historic Buildings (Tower of London), https://blog.hrp.org.uk/curators/the-cardinal-who-stole-christmas/ (2015)
3. Fictionalised interview adapted from Charles Nicholl, *The Reckoning* (Vintage, 2002).

Chapter 9: Travel

1. Fictionalised interview adapted from the author's own lecture 'Travel in the Stuart Age'.
2. My thanks go to Philip Roberts, friend, author and member of the Mary Rose Trust for sending me the text of his book, *The Mary*

Rose in a Nutshell, which is no longer in print, sadly, but has proved to be a goldmine of information.
3. Fictionalised interview adapted from A.L. Rowse, *The First Colonists – Hakluyt's Voyages to North America* (The Folio Society, 1986).
4. https://www.cambridge.org/core/journals/renaissance-quarterly/article/philip-sidneys-travels-in-the-holy-roman-empire/7B8A0B476A9FEE5E2F5B78E2F96AF447

Chapter 10: Leisure Time

1. Fictionalised interview from the notes and text in John Gassner (ed), *Medieval and Tudor Drama,* (Applause Theatre Book Publishers, 1987).
2. The complete text can be found at https://www.presscom.co.uk/halliwell/baldwin/baldwin_1584.html
3. https://moneyweek.com/421338/11-january-1569-england-holds-its-first-lottery-draw
4. Don't blame me if this confuses you utterly. I couldn't understand the game at all and took the liberty of copying this text from http://jan.ucc.nau.edu/~wew/Tattershall-tb/dice.html
5. It's suggested that the game was also called Pope Julius, but the Protestants renamed it Pope Joan as a joke, referring to the legend that the Pope who reigned from 855–857/8 was actually an English woman – a story vehemently denied by the Roman Catholic Church and yet there is, intriguingly, a two-and-a-half-year gap in the list of popes between Benedict III, who was expelled from office in September 855, and the election of Nicholas I, in April 858. An old but intriguing book about Pope Joan, if you want to read more, is *The She-Pope* by Peter Stansford, 1999.
6. https://www.brewershall.co.uk/public-news/the-brewers-book-of-william-porlond/
7. http://www.graveshamtrophycentre.com/pages/131-tudors-football-history-1500-50

List of Illustrations

1. King Richard III – National Portrait Gallery, wikicommons public domain
2. Henry VII – NPG, wikicommons public domain
3. Lady Margaret Beaufort – NPG, wikicommons public domain
4. Henry VIII – Museo Nacional Thyssen-Bornemisza, wikicommons public domain
5. Edward VI – NPG, wikicommons public domain
6. Lady Jane Grey – NPG, wikicommons public domain
7. Mary I – Museo del Prado, wikicommons public domain
8. Elizabeth I – NPG, wikicommons public domain
9. St Bartholomew the Great's Church (interior) – photo GRM
10. Thomas Harman's pamphlet, 'A Caveat or Warning for Common Cursitors', 1567 – British Library, wikicommons public domain
11. Ightham Mote, National Trust, Kent – photo GRM
12. Henry VII Sovereign (obverse) – Cleveland Museum of Art, wikicommons public domain
13. Sir Thomas Gresham, circa 1565 – NPG, wikicommons public domain
14. Cardinal Wolsey's statue in Ipswich, Suffolk – photo GRM
15. Detail Woodcut of 'Typographus Der Buchdrucker' (The Printer), 1568, Folger, creative commons public domain
16. Thomas Digges' idea of the universe in 'Prognostications Everlasting', 1576 – Wellcome Collection, wikicommons public domain
17. A tally iron – Auckland War Memorial Museum, wikicommons public domain
18. Tudor knot garden at Penshurst Place, Kent – photo GRM

19. John Gerard's illustration of a Virginia Potato, 1596 – Wellcome Collection, wikicommons public domain
20. Lesnes Abbey, Bexley, Kent – photo GRM
21. Portrait of Sir Thomas More – Frick Collection, New York, wikicommons public domain
22. Anglesey Abbey, near Cambridge – photo GRM
23. Ripon Cathedral Rood Screen, North Yorkshire – photo Diliff, wikimedia creative commons public domain
24. Sugar Loaf, Sutton House, NT, London – photo GRM
25. 'Family Saying Grace', attributed to Antoon Claeissens – Hall's Croft Collection via wikimedia commons public domain
26. Gainsborough Old Hall: Kitchen, English Heritage, Lincs – photo Richard Croft via wikimedia creative commons public domain
27. A great mullein plant, at Sissinghurst Castle, NT, Kent – photo GRM
28. Elizabeth I 'Armada Portrait' – Woburn Abbey, via wikimedia creative commons public domain
29. Henry VIII's queens, by kind permission of Tudor Legacies: The Queens of Henry VIII re-enactment group, taken at Penshurst Place, Kent – photo GRM.
30. Elizabeth Knollys, Lady Layton, attributed to George Gower – Montacute House, NT, Somerset, commons wikimedia public domain
31. Queen Elizabeth I, c.1585–90 – NPG, wikimedia commons public domain
32. Sir Walter Raleigh oval portrait by Nicholas Hilliard – NPG, wikimedia commons public domain
33. Henry VIII after Hans Holbein the Younger – Walker Art Gallery, wikimedia commons public domain
34. 'Unknown Man in a Red Doublet' by Hans Eworth – Musée des Beaux Arts de Besançon, wikimedia commons public domain
35. An unidentified man thought to be Ralph Sadlier by Hans Holbein the Younger – Royal Collection, wikimedia commons public domain
36. Family of Henry VIII c.1545 (detail) – Hampton Court Palace, wikimedia commons public domain

37. Natural Silk-sponges as contraceptives and tampons – photo GRM
38. Robert Dudley Earl of Leicester – Waddesdon Manor, wikimedia creative commons public domain
39. Ightham Mote, NT, Kent – photo GRM
40. Ruins of Scadbury Manor, Chislehurst, Kent – photo Ethan Doyle White wikimedia creative commons public domain
41. Sir Francis Walsingham by John De Critz the Elder – NPG, wikicommons public domain
42. Mary, Queen of Scots by François Clouet – Royal Collection, wikicommons public domain
43. Roderigo Lopez by E. Hulsius – Wellcome Images, wikimedia commons public domain
44. Christopher Marlowe, British School – Corpus Christi College, Cambridge wikimedia commons public domain
45. World map circa 1510 by Martin Waldseemüller (1470–1520) – Library of Congress wikimedia commons public domain
46. Warrior of the Secotan Indians in North Carolina by John White, 1585 – British Museum, wikimedia commons public domain
47. Baron's Hall, Penshurst Place, Kent – photo GRM
48. Penshurst Place in Kent – Birthplace of Sir Philip Sidney – photo GRM
49. Sir Philip Sidney after Antonis Mor – NPG wikicommons public domain
50. Shakespeare's historical tragedy Richard III, 1594 – Folger Shakespeare Library creative commons public domain
51. The first page of *Beware the Cat!* by William Baldwin 1553 – British Library public domain
52. The Pleasant Game of the Goose – MET, New York wikicommons public domain
53. 'Four Gentlemen of High Rank Playing Primero', circle of Master of the Countess of Warwick – private collection The Earl of Derby, wikicommons public domain

54. Pope Joan Board – Project Gutenberg, wikicommons public domain
55. Scottish football found at Stirling Castle – The Stirling Smith Art Gallery and Museum public domain
56. 'Elizabeth I Playing the Lute' *c.*1580 by Nicholas Hilliard – Private Collection, wikicommons public domain

Suggested Further Reading

John Gassner (ed), *Medieval and Tudor Drama,* (Applause Theatre Book Publishers, 1987).

Ruth Goodman, *How to be a Tudor,* (Penguin, 2015).

Adam Hart-Davis, *What the Tudors & Stuarts Did for Us* (Boxtree, 2002).

Suzannah Lipscomb, *A Visitor's Companion to Tudor England*, (Ebury Press, 2012).

Toni Mount, *Everyday Life in Medieval London,* (Amberley, 2014) – includes early Tudors.

Toni Mount, *Medieval Medicine – Its Mysteries and Science,* (Amberley, 2016) – includes Tudor medicine.

Charles Nicholl, *The Reckoning*, (Vintage, 2002) – on Christopher Marlowe.

Stephen Porter, *Everyday Life in Tudor London,* (Amberley Publishing, Glos, 2016).

A. L. Rowse, *The First Colonists – Hakluyt's Voyages to North America*, (The Folio Society, 1986).

Alison Sim, *The Tudor Housewife,* (Sutton Publishing, Glos, 1996).

Hilary Spurling, *Elinor Fettiplace's Receipt Book – Elizabethan Country House Cooking,* (Viking Salamander, 1986).

Alison Weir, *The Six Wives of Henry VIII*, (Vintage Books Ltd. Paperback version, 2007).

Acknowledgements

My special thanks go to my friends Sandi Lowring and Phil Roberts. Sandi provided me with a wealth of information and anecdotes on Ightham Mote, Kent, where she is a National Trust volunteer. Phil sent me a PDF of his book about the *Mary Rose* which is no longer available but proved a mine of information. Phil will shortly be releasing (or probably has released by now) a biography of Cardinal Wolsey, published by Pen and Sword that I know is well worth reading, having had a preview.

Elizabeth (Bess) Chilver's help was invaluable as she edited my chapter on Tudor fashion and put me right about numerous aspects, from make-up to footwear. I owe her so much. I truly appreciate all that she has done to help me in getting the facts right while keeping the light-hearted tone. Thank you, Bess, for all your time and trouble.

I have to thank my husband Glenn for his photography, taking me to various Tudor venues for research purposes and generally being indispensable when I need IT assistance, a quick fact-check or another cup of coffee. I couldn't do without his support.

Thanks also go to those at Pen and Sword, including Claire Hopkins and Alan Murphy, since without them this book would not be in your hands now.

Index

A Plain and Easy Introduction to Practical Music 178
Act of Supremacy 55, 57
Acts of Apparel 85, 100,
Anglesey Abbey, Cambs 59
Anne Boleyn, Queen 11, 13, 28, 36-7, 39, 54-5, 58, 66, 83, 88-90, 108, 110-2, 124, 159, 171
Anne of Cleves, Queen 75, 91, 112-3
Arthur, Prince of Wales 83

Babington, Anthony 131-2, 136, 139
Baldwin, William 164-6
Bankside, Southwark 162
Barclay, Alexander 174
Barre, Helen/Ellen 105
Barre, Matthew 106-7
Battle of Bosworth 2-3
Battle of Flodden 114
Battle of Hastings 1-2
Battle of the Spurs 124
Battle of Zutphen 157
Beaufort, Lady Margaret 8-9, 100
Beggars 20-1

Beware the Cat! 164-5
Boleyn, George, Earl of Rochford 91, 109
Boleyn, Thomas, Earl of Wilshire 124-5
Bond of Association 130, 133
Book of Common Prayer 62
Book of Psalms 62
Boorde, Andrew 70-3
Brandon, Charles, Duke of Suffolk 83
Bridewell, London, House of Correction 23
Bristol 74, 142
Burbage, James 162
Burbage, Richard 162
Byland Abbey, Yorks 65

Cambridge University 36, 46, 48, 62, 128, 134, 136-7, 151
Campion, Edmund 68
Carew, Sir George 145
Carlisle Castle, Cumbria 175
Caxton, William 7, 37, 77
Cecil, Robert 134-6, 140
Cecil, William, Lord Burghley 127, 152-3

Index

Charles IX, King of France 120
Christmas 72, 74, 126-7, 165, 167-8, 177, 181
Chronicle 126
Church of England 12, 46, 55, 113, 134
Clement, Sir Richard, Gentleman Usher 28-9, 123-5
Columbus, Christopher 84
Copernicus, Nicolaus 42-3, 48
Cornysh, William 177
Coverdale, Miles 61-2
Cranmer, Thomas, Archbishop of Canterbury 62, 65
Cromwell, Thomas, Earl of Essex 11, 37, 54, 58, 61, 105-6, 123
Culpepper, Joyce 114
Culpepper, Thomas 112

Danby, William 139
Dare, Ananias 150
Dare/White, Eleanor 150
Daubeney, Sir Giles 35
De Bourbon, Charlotte 156
De Revolutionibus 42-3
De Valois, Henry, Duke of Anjou 120
De Vere, Edward, Earl of Oxford 93
Dee, Dr John 39, 146, 151-54
Deptford, SE London 125, 139-140

Devereux, Robert, Earl of Essex 134-6, 157
Digges, Leonard 43-5
Digges, Thomas 43
Dissolution of the Monasteries 19, 21, 55-6, 59, 106
Dom Antonio of Portugal 134-5
Drake, Sir Francis 147, 157
Dudley, Edmund 9, 12, 123
Dudley, Guildford 13-4, 117
Dudley, John, Duke of Northumberland 12-3
Dudley, Robert, Earl of Leicester 16, 51, 89, 118-9, 122, 134, 152, 155, 157
Duke of Alençon 157
Dyetary of Health 70

Edward IV 4
Edward VI 9, 11-2, 23, 31, 46, 62-3, 106, 152, 164-5, 181
Elizabeth I 10, 16, 26, 39, 94, 177
Eltham Palace 126
Empson, Richard 9, 123
Enclosures 18-9
Eric XVI, King of Sweden 120

Fettiplace, Lady Elinor 79
Field of the Cloth of Gold 30, 105
FitzAlan, Henry Earl of Arundel 118
Fleet Prison 125

Fotheringhay Castle, Northants 133
Francis I, King of France 11, 30
Francis, Jacques, salvage diver 22
Frith, Mary, aka Moll Cut-Purse 143
Frizer, Ingram 139-40

Gainsborough Old Hall, Lincs 81
Galileo 41
Gerard, John 49, 51-2
Gibbons, Orlando 177
Gifford 131-2, 136
Golden Hind 147
Grammar/King's Schools 46, 48
Greenwich Palace 103
Gregory XIII, Pope 68
Gresham, Sir Thomas 31, 33-4, 48
Grey, Lady Anne 28
Guildford, Sir Edward 125

Habsburg, Emperor Charles V 11
Hackney, London 105-6
Hakluyt, Richard 26, 147, 149
Hall, Edward 126
Hamilton, James, Earl of Arran 118
Hamlet 162
Hampton Court Palace 28, 35-7, 52, 85
Harman, Thomas 23
Harold II 1-2

Henry VII; Henry Tudor 2-4, 6-8, 9-10, 13, 53, 83, 91, 97, 119, 123, 163, 167, 170
Henry VIII 1, 9-13, 20, 22, 28-31, 35, 39, 47, 49, 53-8, 60-3, 70, 72, 74-6, 80, 83, 86, 89, 91, 97-100, 102, 105-6, 108-9, 111-4, 117-8, 123-8, 145, 166-7, 170-1, 174-6
Herbal or General Historie of Plantes 51
Hever Castle, Kent 83, 112, 124
Heywood, John 160
Hilliard, Nicholas 34, 95, 177
Holinshed, Ralph 9
Homily of Good Works 63
Howard, Edmund 114
Howard, Thomas, 2nd Duke of Norfolk 114
Howard, Thomas, 3rd Duke of Norfolk 112

Ightham Mote, Kent 27-8, 124
Inflation 19, 26, 30
Ireland 26, 105-6, 154
Isle of Wight 22, 145

James VI/I, King of Scots and England 40-1, 62, 142, 154
Jane Grey, Queen 13-4, 89, 117, 119
Jane Seymour, Queen 91, 111
Jennings, Nicholas, aka Blunt 23-6
John-John, Tib and Sir John 160

Index

Katherine Howard, Queen 91, 112
Katherine of Aragon, Queen 11-2, 28, 36, 54, 65, 83, 91, 108, 127, 171
Katherine Parr Queen 86, 91, 113
Kelley, Edward 153
Kenilworth Castle, Warwickshire 51, 120
Knole, Archbishop of Canterbury's residence 124
Knollys, Elizabeth, Lady Layton 92
Knollys, Sir Francis 175
Knollys/Dudley, Lettice 122
Kyd, Thomas 138

Leland, John 160
Leo X, Pope 35, 53
Lesnes Abbey, SE London 56
Lily's Grammar 47
Lollard 9, 61
Lopes, Dr Rodrigo 134
Lydgate, John 77

Malory, Sir Thomas 7
Marlowe, Christopher/Kit 137, 139-40
Mary Tudor, Queen 9, 87, 154, 162
Mary, Queen of Scots 127, 130, 133, 175, 177
Mayne, Cuthbert 68
Mendoza, Spanish Ambassador 130

Mercator, Gerard 145-6
More, Sir Thomas, Chancellor 20, 57, 61, 159
Morley, Thomas 178
Morte d'Arthur 7
Mulcaster, Richard 175

National lottery 166
Nonesuch Palace 30
Norton, Thomas 67
Norwich 142

Oxford University 35

Peckham, George 26
Penshurst Place, Kent 50, 124, 154-5
Perez, Antonio 135
Petty Schools 46
Philip II, King of Spain 15, 130, 134-6
Philips, Thomas 131
Phillips, Henry 61
Pickering, Sir William 118
Pius V, Pope 67, 128
Plantagenets 2, 4, 8
Poley, Robert 139-40
Poor Rate 23
Porlond, William 174
Potatoes 52, 74, 79, 151
Prague University 151
Pratt, Thomas 168
Princes in the Tower 4-5
Prognostication everlasting 43-4

193

Raleigh, Sir Walter 40, 74, 85, 95, 98, 144, 148-51
Ralph Roister Doister 160-1
Reformation 6, 46, 55-6, 65, 72
Richard III 2-4, 6, 29, 159, 164
Richmond Palace 112, 126, 167
Roanoke, North Carolina 148-50
Robsart/Dudley, Amy 119
Roman Catholic Church 11, 42, 54, 60, 118
Rombaud, Jean 109-10
Rudolf II, Holy Roman Emperor 153
Russell, John 77

Sadleir, Sir Ralph 105, 107, 132
Sandwich, Kent 98
Scadbury Manor, Chislehurst, Kent 128-9, 139
Seymour, Edward, Duke of Somerset 12
Seymour, Thomas 113
Shakespeare, William 7-8, 47, 137, 159, 163-4
Sidney, Sir Henry 154
Sidney, Sir Philip 154, 158-9
Sidney/Dudley, Lady Mary 85
Skeres, Nicholas 139-40
Smallpox 83-5
Spenser, Edmund 156
St Augustine's Church, Hackney, London 106
St Mary-at-Hill Church, London 65

St Bartholomew's Day massacre 155
St Bartholomew's Hospital, London 21, 134
St George's Chapel, Windsor 112
St Nicholas Church, Deptford 140
St Paul's Cathedral 64, 66-7, 158, 162, 166
St Peter ad Vincula Chapel, Tower of London 112
St Thomas's Hospital, Southwark 23
Stirling Castle, Scotland 176
Stow, John 33-4, 49
Strickland, William 74
Stubbs, Philip 49
Sudeley Castle, Glos 86, 113
Sugar 71, 78-81
Surveyor of the Highway 141-2
Sweating sickness 3, 83
Syphilis 83-4, 115, 135

Table Manners for Children 77
The Bible 9, 53, 56, 60, 62, 130
The Boke of Keruinge 77
The Brick Place 105-6
The Complete Gamester 169
The Faerie Queene 156
The Globe theatre 163
The Lives of the Caesars 47
The Mary Rose, flagship 30, 145
The Netherlands 109, 138, 145, 157

Index

The Private Life of Henry VIII 75
The Silver Swan 177
The Tragedy of Gorboduc 67
Third and Last Book of Songs 178
Throckmorton, Francis 68, 130
Tobacco 40, 85-6, 144, 151
Tower of London 15-6, 34, 41, 57, 67, 89, 109, 112, 119
Treaty of Tordesillas 148
Tunstall, Cuthbert, Bishop of London 60
Turkey 72, 74-5
Tyburn Hill, London 68, 136
Tyndale, William 60-2

Udell, Nicholas 160-1

Van den Plass, Dinghen 49, 94
Victoria, Queen 1
Virginia, America 26, 51-2, 148

Walsingham, Sir Francis 127-35, 138-9
Walsingham, Thomas 139
Wareham, William, Archbishop of Canterbury 124
Westminster Abbey 28, 112, 124
White, John 148-9
Whitehall Palace 67
Wittlebury, Anne 28
William the Conqueror 1
William the Silent of Orange 156
Winchester Cathedral 118
Windsor Castle 112, 120
Wolsey, Thomas, Archbishop of York 28, 35-7, 48, 54, 123, 126, 128, 189
Worde, Wynkyn de 37, 77
Wylgres, Edward 168

York 142